Autograph Page

_____

_____

_____

_____

_____

PREFACE

In this book, I will describe some of the things that go on behind the barbed-wire gates and concrete walls and inside the police precincts, county jails and state penitentiaries. Although it does not refer to the federal correctional facilities, some of the information may still apply. The prison industry in the United States is one of the largest industries and has become a billion-dollar enterprise.

Prison was originally designed to hold or detain the accused until they made either bail and were released on bond or had their day in court or to house those convicted of their crimes. Initially, you're presumed innocent until you're proven guilty beyond a reasonable doubt, or you enter into a plea agreement, which could be in your best interest depending on your circumstances. I will discuss these issues in depth later on in the book.

Prison today has evolved into big business. That's right. It's a government entity that warehouses people who have not only broken laws that govern the land but also who have merely violated them but did not have sufficient funds to obtain adequate legal representation. The corrections industry is becoming so vast that even private corporations are building and managing prisons to secure a piece of the pie.

Unfortunately, the prison industry is growing rapidly and it's at the expense of our friends, family and neighbors. Either directly or indirectly, we are all affected, whether family, friends, offenders or taxpayers.

The United States incarcerates more people than any other country in the world. Currently, 2.3 million people are incarcerated in the United States, with more than a million on probation or parole. Over 90 percent of prisoners are men and approximately 50 percent are African American, 20 percent are of Latin descent, and 30 percent are Caucasian.

I don't have a formal degree in law and this book is not an official legal guide. But I was introduced to the penal system at a very early age and this book gives an honest account of my experience first-hand!

I hope that by sharing this information, I can help someone gain a better understanding of what goes on in prison. And maybe then they will think twice before committing a crime, or maybe they will be deterred altogether.

It's important to remember that when you go to prison, you're not the only one who suffers. It affects your loved ones, family members, friends, neighbors, employers, and your community.

Do you have room in your life for prison? Probation?

Parole? Do you know someone who needs to break the destructive cycle before they commit a crime or become a victim? Then read on…

101 THINGS YOU SHOULD KNOW ABOUT JAIL

BONUS CHAPTER: 50 questions you should ask anyone returning home from Prison

Timeless Thomas

101 Things You Should Know About Jail

By Daron Swann

Cover Design by Daron Swann

Logo Designs by LeRoy Grayson

Editor: Anelda L. Attaway

ISBN 978-1-954425-52-1

Library of Congress Control Number: 2022910830

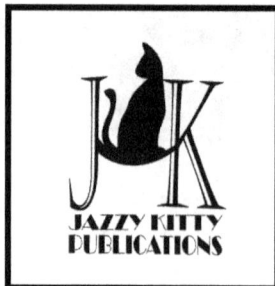

JAZZY KITTY
PUBLICATIONS

TABLE OF CONTENTS

INTRODUCTION

Okay. Let's cut to the chase.

You find yourself in the back seat of a police car with those metal bracelets snugly locked around your wrists. Or even worse, your hands are hog-tied behind your back with plastic ties designed for binding bundles of newspapers.

Either you've made a mistake and have been caught, or it's a case of mistaken identity and you're stuck with the burden of having to prove your innocence. Whatever the case, you're on your way to the precinct and you're about to be booked, processed, fingerprinted and strip-searched.

Sometime between the time of the arrest and just before the search, the arresting officer or an officer at the precinct should advise you of your Miranda Rights. These include the right to remain silent; anything you say can and will be used against you in a court of law; you have the right to have an attorney present during questioning; if you cannot afford an attorney, one will be appointed to you.

The severity of your offense will determine whether you are charged with a felony or a misdemeanor. And the charge will

i

determine the type of bail that is set: secured or unsecured. Secured bail means you're going to need money or property to pay your bond. An unsecured bond usually indicates that the offense is not major and you are able to sign out, giving only your word—not money or property—that you will show up for court.

If you are charged with a felony such as rape, robbery, murder, manslaughter, etc., the police will probably insist on interrogating you. Even though your Miranda Rights specifically say, "you have a right to remain silent" or "you have the right to have your attorney present during questioning," the police are trained to deliver the Miranda quickly.

You've seen how it goes in these interrogations if you watch cop shows. And thanks to reality TV, you can get a close and personal view of the tactics officers use during questioning. Mind you, officers are well trained to do what they do, and if you are not properly conditioned to ride the tidal wave, you will sink! If you've committed a crime or have been accused of doing so with one or more persons, these other people will become your co-defendants. They also have the burden of proving their innocence as well—and this is when things can become ugly.

As you've witnessed on TV during interrogations, the police usually play both parties against each other by using one of the oldest tricks in the books—he said, she said. Each defendant is placed in a separate room and the mind games begin. "Joe already told me that you did it, John, so save yourself and tell us what happened." At that same time, another officer is in the room with Joe telling him the same thing about John.

This tactic is one of the swiftest ways to provoke emotion, usually anger and confusion, and has been known to be so effective that not only does it cause one to tell all, but it also shatters friendships and relationships.

The sense of betrayal is gut-wrenching, especially if it is a new experience or foreign to you. This tactic does work and usually—whoever breaks first is the one to get the better deal. But sometimes, that better deal comes with the label of snitch, informant, rat, etc.

That was a crash course in how co-defendants get interrogated and interviewed, but an actual live interrogation is much more involved.

But what's it like when it's only you at the precinct or police station?

Consider that you've just been extracted from society by an officer (or officers). Perhaps they were in police cars with lights flashing, bullhorns bellowing, Tazor guns, pepper spray, black jacks, handguns or who knows what other weapons. Between the flashing light show, blaring sirens and individuals running around you dressed like superheroes, it's quite normal to experience a panic or anxiety attack.

Okay. You've been locked up, read your Miranda Rights and now you're being officially detained for booking and processing. You're in a holding cell/tank with others experiencing the same scenario with different circumstances, of course. It's fair to say that at this juncture, you're on an emotional roller-coaster, and as far as you know, your immediate future is uncertain.

You wait dumbfounded for 45 minutes, an hour, or more to speak with someone and find out the status of your situation, which might go like this: If things aren't too busy and backed up, you can usually get the one phone call you are entitled to, but I've seen times when individuals do not receive that phone call for a variety of reasons. But most of the time, minor offenders have no problem getting their call.

Major offenders or those who have been accused generally are more likely to miss that initial phone call at the precinct. That's because depending on how the interrogation goes, it will set the tempo for the officers' willingness to work with you in that area. And, although it's not right, that's just the way it is. If this does, in fact, happen to you, you'll get your call when you get to the county jail. When they finally pull you out of that germ-infested holding tank and put you in an interview room and handcuff one of your hands to a metal stool that's usually connected to a metal desk that sits directly in front of you, the cop that just cuffed you to the stool then flips personalities. He becomes this mean, aggressive, verbally abusive individual who is in authority, and he begins to manipulate and make every attempt to sway you in the direction of volunteering as much information as you will. Mind you, he doesn't know all the details of the crime in question; he just made the arrest or read the report. Each piece of information you volunteer will be used to build a case against you in court. That's why it's so important to exercise your right to remain silent and your right to have your attorney present during questioning. In other words, SHUT UP!

During the interrogation, the "bad" cop has just grinded you up real good. He walks out of the room for a minute. His partner enters the room. He's the "good" cop. He starts speaking to you with respect and treating you with dignity. Your experience so far has been so horrific that, at this point, you feel like you could use a friend. But he's a wolf in sheep's clothing.

He assures you that it's in your best interest to cooperate with him. In short, he is basically asking you to snitch on yourself, confess to the crime, make it easy on the criminal justice system, and don't have your day in court.

The day has been unending, you're getting tired and hungry, and you're still uncertain about exactly what to do. The choice is yours.

When you get to the county jail, here's what happens. This is the first of 101 things you should know about jail.

CHAPTER ONE

You've just been transported from the precinct to the county jail and your bail has been set. But you can't afford to post bail or bond.

You're now in another holding tank, except this one is a lot more crowded than the one at the precinct. This holding tank is part of the receiving and processing area of the county jail.

It is comprised of people who have come to jail from various precincts—from the homeless to Mr. Upscale. There are always informants in these tanks as well because the case they just caught gave them a reality check-up from the neck up and they are now realizing that they are not prepared to do the time. Here you should keep your mouth shut and never discuss your case/charges/offenses with anyone outside of your attorney.

Most holding tanks are very small. Some are as small as 12 feet x 12 feet with standing room only—maybe sitting room. All of these people confined in these tanks are required to use the one toilet that's in the tank. That's right! Everyone shares the same throne with absolutely no privacy.

Sometimes you are housed in a holding tank for several days before they find a housing unit to send you to. And while three people may be removed, they may lock up 10 more, so it's always crowded in the holding tank of the county jail.

Corrections Officers and Processing

Officers at the county jail are corrections officers, more commonly referred to as COs. After COs are finished processing your paperwork, they will call your name and begin processing you. This entails you to a 2-3 minute shower while they search your personal clothes, shoes, and your body. Afterward, you will receive your uniform.

Sometimes, if you're lucky, you will get new clothes; other times, you'll just have to take what they give you. Some counties allow you to wear your own sneakers; others will provide them for you. During processing, you will be fingerprinted again and given a personal identification number. This number will be your new name during your entire stay in prison for that sentence.

Now that you're processed, you'll probably get to make a phone call. Remember to be careful what you say; all phones are monitored.

Medical Department

Now the medical department will send a representative to interview you to ascertain your medical and psychological histories to determine the accurate treatment plan for you. Most jails have a $5-$6 co-pay for medical services unless your ailment is chronic. Chronic care is free.

There is a negative reflection on prison medical care, but in all actuality, they do what they can with the resources they're allotted. They try their best to keep you healthy. After all, the jail can't make any money off of a dead man.

Classification and Housing

Next, someone will interview you from the Classification Department. This interview is very significant because what you say, combined with your criminal history, will determine what block you're house on.

Special Needs Unit

If you are mentally ill or developmentally disabled, you will be housed on a Special Needs Unit (SNU). There you will be away from the general population and monitored by the psychology and psychiatry staff, as well as supervised a bit more by the COs due to the high suicide rate or violent nature of these inmates.

Mentally ill prisoners are known to be mistreated by staff because their credibility doesn't hold much weight, their voices are virtually silenced, and some of the COs are not properly qualified to deal with them.

They are often denied privileges, such as phone calls and recreation. But it can become as serious as denying them their rights under the Eighth Amendment of the Constitution, which signifies "cruel and unusual punishment." Some of the rights they are denied include showers, meals, or clean clothes and linen. Sometimes, they're even abused.

Maximum Security

If your arrest was too violent and/or your criminal/prison history too extensive, and you're thought to be a threat to the normal operation of the jail, you will be classified to the Maximum Security block/unit.

Maximum Security means you'll be in solitary confinement, locked in a 12-foot x 9-foot cell for 23 hours a day all by yourself. You are allowed out of your cell for only one hour each day to exercise or to walk around in this tiny courtyard that's connected to the cellblock with cameras everywhere and, of course, you're escorted everywhere by a guard. Depending on how you're perceived, you might be handcuffed and shackled around your ankles during your hour of exercise.

When you're in this predicament, it's natural to stress because you're uncertain about how your court case is going to turn out and you're living in deplorable conditions. (To deal with this situation, some find books to read or do a lot of writing.) But the walls of the cells close in on you and you may find it necessary to seek some type of medication to help you deal with the confinement. Until you're in that situation for days or months, you can't possibly imagine how difficult an experience it is.

If there's nothing particularly significant about your situation, you will be classified to one of the jail's general population housing blocks or units.

Protective Custody

If you are about to turn states evidence against someone, you will be placed on a protective custody (PC) unit. Inmates will refer to PC as Punk City or Pussy City. You can also become classified to PC if you have a known enemy in that jail or you're in a gang that's not ruled by the majority. Or, you can end up in PC if you request to be placed there because you aren't cut from the same cloth as the rest of the hardened criminals who reside there and you are afraid.

A number of sex offenders take the PC route, and most of the time, it's for good reasons. No one likes a sex offender. And to provide them with much-needed protection, they can be classified to PC. PC lockup hours and recreation are the same as Maximum Security: 23 hours in your cell and one hour out of it.

Dormitory

You can also be assigned to the dorm. It's a room about as large as a gymnasium, similar to a homeless shelter. There is no privacy in the dorms because you live with between 80-100 inmates who see and hear your every move.

Administrative Segregation

The final classification is administrative segregation, which is also 23 hours in and one hour out. It's common for inmates who are involved in high-profile cases to be housed there. They also classify people who hold real power or rank among peers, such as gang leaders, religious leaders and other individuals that can influence groups of prisoners and sway their thinking. To ensure security, the administration will place these types of individuals in administrative segregation.

General Population

Welcome to general population! A normal county jail block can house anywhere from 100 to 200 inmates. The block is managed by Central Control or block officers. There is a protective bubble-like room where block officers control the doors, lights and televisions. You enter the block with your uniform on and a bag of county-issued supplies, including a toothbrush, toothpaste, soap, toilet paper, and possibly a razor, depending on which jail you're in.

If you had any money on your person at the time of your arrest, it will be placed on your jail account, better known as "the books."

Your family and friends can also send you money. The majority of jails deal with money orders only. You need money to go to the jail's grocery store, known as the commissary.

On the Block

You've just been buzzed in on your new block. You're the new guy and, believe me, it's all eyes on you! People are watching you like a hawk—looking at the way you walk, your facial expressions, and for any sign of weakness so that they can figure out how they're going to go about dealing with you. Strength always detects strength and weakness detects weakness. Being thorough is a universal trait. However, this assessment can only be made after you show and prove what you're about.

On the block, you'll find metal tables and chairs that are welded to the floor. There's a television for the block to watch, which usually sets high or is mounted up high on the wall. On the block is also a "day room," and during the hours the day room is open, inmates hang out there.

Day room activities consist of playing cards, board games, and arts and crafts. Does it remind you of anything? If you were thinking child's play, you're absolutely correct! The games are issued by the jail to each block and designed to pacify the prisoners and help them pass the time away.

This is also a method that distracts prisoners from seeking any true education or higher learner. The jail term for this is "rocking you to sleep." If you don't have a high school diploma or GED, some jails will allow you to participate in classes. Others will make you wait until you are sentenced. Sentenced inmates get many more opportunities and/or privileges than those that are not sentenced.

You must walk from the front door of the block to your cell, which can be somewhat uncomfortable depending on how sure you are of your abilities and how secure you feel in this type of environment.

Most county jails are overcrowded and house three people to cells designed to hold one person. You can very easily be the third wheel in which case you would probably have to sleep on a mattress that is located on the floor next to the bunk beds in a 12 foot x 9 foot cell. This literally leaves no walking space and limits movement altogether. All three cellmates share the same sink and toilet facilities located in the cell. It's fair to say that you're crammed in like sardines.

If you're fortunate, you can land in a cell where there is only one other person. At the time you meet your new cellmate, the first real test begins. It's no question that the bottom bunk will go to the one who demonstrates superiority, either by demeanor or by action. I've even seen some get verbally finessed out of the bottom bunk.

The reason this test is so significant is because once you unpack your stuff and make your bed, the nosey vultures on the block get to see how you handle your cellmate(s) and can begin to assess the role you might be about to play as a whole. That's because the block is a community and everyone plays a role, even if your role is to stay out of the way. By the way, nosey people are referred to as "ear hustlers" and "eye hustlers"—a terminology used to describe those whose senses are extremely heightened—which is a good quality to have in prison. It can mean the difference between making a good or bad decision.

Now once you unpack your personal belongs and establish your position, you will be placed among the prisoners in an unwritten category. For instance, you will be categorized by neighborhood, gang, religion, race, culture, age, loner/outcast, etc. It is best to always display strength because the weak are vulnerable and will, by all means, be taken advantage of.

Let me clear up the things that you've heard about jail for you right now. The rumors and stigmas, they're all true! This is why the "weak" dude is the last dude you want to be.

You're allowed out of your cell, on the block, and in the day room area from 8-10:30 a.m. Then you're locked in your cell until it's time for lunch, around 11 a.m. until about noon, then you're locked back in your cell until count time. Count time is when COs count all inmates in every block and work area to ensure they are all accounted for.

You will be allowed out of your cell again around 1 p.m., after the count clears, to indulge in more day room activities or to go to the courtyard connected to the block. There you can walk around get fresh air and shoot half-court basketball. These activities usually last until 3 p.m. and then it's back to the cell again until about 4:30 or 5 p.m. for dinner. After dinner, you're locked back in your cell until about 6 p.m. and it's day room until 8 or 9 p.m. After that, you're locked in for the rest of the evening. You wake up about 6 a.m. to eat breakfast and are locked back in your cell until 8 a.m. and begin the same routine again.

When you're in a dorm, because you don't have a cell to be locked into, you must remain on your bunk during the select lock-in times. During the rest of the day, you're free to roam the block and invade everyone else's space.

Most county jails have central heating, air conditioning and windows that don't open. Can you imagine the stench that reeks in a dormitory style setting?

Each block has at least one scheduled gym day, sometimes two, and two or three scheduled library days.

Do you have to use the bathroom?

Are you ready to take a shower?

Well, before you do, let me remind you about who you share the block with...

Who's on the Block?

You share the block with people who were not too long ago homeless and sleeping under a cardboard box or in a bus station. There are also vicious drug addicts, some still going through withdrawal. And others have been locked up long enough to have gone through withdrawal. However, their mentality and actions are still that of a substance abuser.

Then you have the dirty pirate/Viking that is unclean and filthy. And there's also the gay and transgendered. You also have some who have mental health issues that were not diagnosed with symptoms strong enough to land them in the Special Needs Unit. The rest of the population is pretty much tidy and makes an effort to keep their areas clean.

All of the people on the block, including yourself, having been removed from society. Now, that doesn't necessarily mean that they are the worst of the worst. It just means that they have been arrested and accused of a crime and detained. The block's day room, bathrooms, and showers are cleaned by block workers. Block workers are inmates from the block who basically perform janitorial duties. Two types of people can get these jobs: those who show strength and are willing to step up to the task, and kiss-asses.

Although these jobs only pay 20-25 cent an hour, some of the other perps make up the difference. Workers can stay out on the block and watch television about an hour later than everyone else who is locked in for the night, and workers are usually out of their cells during other lock-in times. This creates a vehicle for things to get passed from cell-to-cell during lock-ins, securing the worker a percentage even if it's a small one. And last but certainly not least, workers can get extra meals from whatever is left over when meals are served.

By being locked in a jail, or caged in a cell, man is far from his natural habitat. Cages were designed to contain animals and, after spending time in a cage, one can easily become uncivilized.

Once this happens, your savage side can take over and this is exactly what happens to a lot of inmates.

Being taken from modern civilization and thrown in with a bunch of wolves and vultures, I can tell you that sheep don't and won't last. Animalistic behavior begins to become first nature. COs who keep watch bear witness to your current characteristics and have no problem looking down their noses at you and treating you as a second-class citizen. They often treat inmates without any sympathy to their transition from society to prison, which is difficult for most people. Being extracted from your home and everything that you know and love has a major impact not only on you, but also on your loved ones and friends. A wife loses her husband temporarily, a daughter loses her father, a mother and father lose their son, and a sibling loses a brother.

What about your job if you were employed? That counts, too. Your boss will certainly be a man short when you are locked up. It's not only an inconvenience, but also an unfortunate situation for everyone involved.

Now combine that with an open court case and an uncertain outcome. There's no training or counseling to help you deal with your new situation, and you have quite a few accidents waiting to happen. Trust me. There's not a lot of room for trial and error. You're in a different world and you better learn the rules of engagement sooner than later.

Bathrooms and Showers

The bathrooms and showers vary depending on what style of block you are housed on—from dormitory to regular block housing units.

As I mentioned earlier, if you live on a block with cells, then the bathrooms—the sink and toilet—are shared only between you and your cellmates. If you live on the dorm blocks, the bathrooms are very similar to those of the bathrooms in the locker room of a gymnasium. A significant difference, though, is there are no privacy dividers to create stalls. Everything is out in the open. That's right. There is absolutely no privacy when using the bathroom, and that's not even the worst part.

The worst part is there are only about four toilets and five or six sinks, and they are shared by the entire block—anywhere from 80-100 people.

Don't think it could get any worse than that? Well, it can!

Not only do you have to share this community-style bathroom with other inmates who are housed on the block with you, but it's a normal scenario for you to be sitting on the toilet when two or three other guys are standing within three feet of you waiting for you to finish your business so they can handle theirs. Horse stables have smelled better than community bathrooms in jail.

Showers are just as bad, if not worse. There are two different kinds of showers. One has stalls, in which case there is only one man showering at a time. In these stalls, you have some privacy because there is a door or curtain that covers you from your knees up to about your neck, depending on how tall you are. But there are only four to eight of these stalls and they must be shared by the entire block.

Then there's the open shower room set up. This is a weak inmate's nightmare, a freak inmate's playground, and a gay inmate's heaven. There can be anywhere from three to five shower heads and that many inmates showering at one time. Some inmates shower in their underwear. Others shower completely nude because they are either well-endowed or seek attention. And there are transgendered inmates who have been taking hormones, and had surgery, silicone enhancements and Botox injections that make them look like real women from the waist up.

It's best to keep your eyes to yourself when showering in these types of open showers because making eye contact could open up opportunities for someone to make advances. It's been said that, "the same size your penis is when you get into the shower is the same size it should be when you get out of the shower." In other words, there should be nothing arousing about taking showers around other men. And sometimes, although men weren't into homosexuality in society, after being locked away for a while, they fall victim to their weaknesses and give into temptation and the evils that men do. This generally happens when you see men showering together regularly or staying in the showers well after everyone has left. Young inmates new to jail or the system can easily be taken advantage of. Put these smells together: sperm, blood, sweat, tears and poop. That's what rape smells like! If you think that was awkward imagine the folks who have been conditioned to accept this as a norm.

Your stature doesn't really matter as long as you show strength and stand up for yourself, they'll leave you alone and move along to other possible victims.

WELCOME TO COUNTY!

Welcome to County Jail!

CHAPTER TWO

CO Ranks and Qualifications

The ranks of correctional officers (COs/prison guards) are set up similar to the military. For instance, it ranges from CO to corporal, sergeant, lieutenant, captain, major, deputy warden, and warden.

A large number of COs were probably bullied growing up. As COs, they have an opportunity to turn the tables and are in a position to retaliate on those who remind them of those who, perhaps, made their lives miserable when they were kids. A smaller number are really in it from the heart. They're higher ups who've earned their stripes through years of dedication to enforcing every rule that is written in the manual—and some!

With the burgeoning of the prison population, the system was forced to hire new guards who have minimum qualifications to police the jails. Age and educational requirements for COs were 18 years of age or older with a high school education or GED (no felonies, of course).

Working in the prison system as a CO is a career with benefits. And the tasks included require much more education than is currently required. The job requires being able to multi- task, deal with other people's issues, use some psychology to assist those incarcerated, be professional, and have good 'ol common sense, which some people just don't have. It doesn't require bringing personal problems into a work environment that is already filled with problems.

But many who aren't qualified to deal with this type of position are hired. They keep watch over prisoners even though some may have more baggage than those they are hired to oversee, which results in organized confusion.

Older COs—both male and female—who have worked in the system so long and have seen and done it all are at a point in their careers that, if you show them respect and stay out of their way, they will stay out of yours.

The COs working in county jails live within the city limits and neighboring areas around the jail. In other words, they're locals so it's highly possible for an inmate to know a CO from the community. Now, knowing COs prior to going to the jail where they work can increase your chances of participating in the black market.

CO Chain of Command

Of course, there's a chain of command. The entry-level COs answer to their corporal or sergeant. Sergeants answer to their lieutenants, the lieutenants to their captains, the captains to their majors, and their majors to the deputy wardens. The deputy wardens report to the warden.

If you need to go even higher up the chain of command, you can contact assistance from Central Office to the governor's office.

Male COs

Male COs have many different personalities. Some have a real hard-nosed mentality. Several bring a military background to the table. Others have a chip on their shoulder for whatever reason. Some gun to move up in rank at any expense. Some are so incompetent that you wonder how they ever landed the job in the first place. Others are plainly holding on to that "I was bullied" mentality and haven't begun to deal with those issues. Others are on the take and control a large percentage of the black market (see page for more information about the black market). Some are just there to do their eight hours and get back home safely. But only a few are fair and empathetic.

Female COs

Female COs are a whole different story.

There are those hard nose, do-it-by-the-book types. There are also those who are experiencing the effects of their monthly cycle and bring emotional instability to the job. You have military, female COs who are trained to spot weakness. And then there are lesbian COs who can't stand men for whatever reason and find delight in being in an authoritative position.

You also have those who strive to reach a higher rank as if to prove they are equally capable of performing the same job as their male counterparts. And those who have experienced abuse look at their position as an opportunity to step on the necks of male inmates. Their issues are clearly unresolved and even though most people could empathize with the pain they have experienced, their misdirected anger can make an inmate's incarceration that much harder.

You have young women who have just been hired and are not only new to the prison system but are also clueless about the caliber of men they'll be working with. Of course, some prisoners are old enough to be their fathers and/or grandfathers. Some are veterans of prison life and others are so institutionalized that they function best when incarcerated. These young female COs are often vulnerable and some end up playing both sides of the fence. With men who are refined, groomed, and built, it's very easy for young female COs to get confused and begin fraternizing with those she is supposed to oversee. Some have even said that "working in a male prison is like being a kid in a candy store." Finally, there are the female COs with low self-esteem because they're obese or don't feel they're pretty. When working at the facility, they get the attention they have never gotten—or probably will never get outside the jail—and it is magnified by one hundred. That's right! That girl who wore thick glasses or was too fat and ugly to get any attention in school now has her time to shine. Inmates will treat her like a queen; all-female COs are beautiful in the eye of an incarcerated man. Whether the attention is genuine or not, these female COs appreciate the attention they receive.

Grievances, Write-ups and Documentation

Most grievances can be handled right inside the jail. However, an occasional negligent act by the jail will pique the interest of civil attorneys and they have no problem taking an inmate's case (on the condition that they don't get paid unless you get paid).

Civil attorneys could care less about the CO's ranking. They deal with representatives from the jail's legal team. And when the case is solid enough that the civil attorney knows he can win, he'll humanize those hard-nose, power-tripping COs who were involved in the case, if any. They say: "Everyone needs a slice of 'humble pie' every now and then."

I can honestly say that a large number of COs enjoy the authority they have over others, and most of them abuse that power. It's back to the saying: "Ain't no fun when the rabbit got the gun"— in short when the tables have turned.

Some of those same individuals who were picked on and mistreated in school now not only have the legal authority to lock the doors behind you, but they can also deny you of privileges, such as phone calls and commissary. They also observe your daily behavior and keep logs on you. When they really want to flex their power, they can write you up for minor or major in-house infractions, which could ultimately result in your going to the "hole"—as if you didn't already have enough troubles already. Just because COs write you up doesn't necessarily mean they are telling the truth. It just means you have been written up and it's up to the hearing examiner to determine your fate. Not only that, these infractions are documented in your file and will follow you throughout your incarceration. The old adages: "Treat others the way you wish to be treated" or "what goes around comes around" doesn't mean a thing now.

CO to Inmate Ratio

Most of the blocks are monitored by only a few COs. A sergeant oversees everything. The block is monitored in three shifts, generally running from 8 a.m.-4 p.m., 4 p.m.-midnight, and midnight-8 a.m. Of course, depending on the jail, some shift schedules are different.

Only a few officers are responsible for the oversight of anywhere from 80 to 150 inmates, sometimes more. Although the inmates are the majority, the administration pretty much keeps things in order by systematically operating the prison in the exact same manner day after day.

Quick Response Teams and Weapons

When disturbances occur on the blocks or other areas of the jail, the Quick Response Teams (QRT) immediately respond to the incident. QRTs are groups of officers who have undergone special training for rioting, fights and other threatening behavior.

When they show up, horns blare, bells ring, and a group of large men—and perhaps a woman or two—dressed like storm troopers from Star Wars with riot gear, helmets, knee and arm pads and the works appear.

These QRT members also carry many weapons, such as shields with electric stun gun power, Tazor guns, pepper spray, tear gas, bean bag rifles or those that shoot rubber and/or salt and pepper pellets.

Other times, the weapons that QRT members carry are needed and well justified when used. Some inmates are very violent and dangerous. Some are crafty and illusive and some have even had prior military experience. Some are hardcore gang members and some are redneck bikers. Some are boxers, wrestlers and/or karate experts, and some are big, husky, former athletes—you know, the type that can beat up three or four guys before five or six men can contain them.

And just because they have the authority to use these weapons and apply the necessary force to get a chaotic situation under control, they don't always act within the guidelines of the Constitution. What's worse is inmates at the county level of their incarceration are not familiar with their rights under this Constitution.

Inmate Rights

One of the biggest misconceptions is that inmates lose all of their rights when they go to prison. It is true that you will lose some rights, especially if you are convicted of a felony. For instance, you can lose your right to vote, bear arms, or even drink alcohol. But as a prisoner in the United States, you are still protected under many other Constitutional Rights.

Inmate Weapons

Inmates have somewhat of an arsenal of their own.

Following are just a few:

Shanks: Homemade knives commonly made from ice- picks, screwdrivers or any other wooden or metal rods.

Extension cords: Used as choking devices.

Socks filled with items. Socks filled with five or six bars of soap, batteries, dominoes, or anything that can be used to smack someone across the head or face.

The Cell Block Atmosphere

The tension on county jail cell blocks is very high. That's mostly because everyone's future is uncertain. This tension creates a lot of unstable thinking, which is why it is so important for you to "get in where you fit in." When everyone stays segregated in their own little group, it allows others to see who they're affiliated with, and the right affiliation can reduce—or even prevent—someone from becoming a target or a mark.

Some inmates are waiting to make bail, some are awaiting their court decisions, and some have just been sentenced and are waiting to be transferred to a state prison. Some are new, young, old, veterans of the system, etc., which creates a hodge-podge of attitudes and atmosphere. Combine these attitudes along with the COs' mentalities and what is supposed to be a routine environment can be very unpredictable.

Contraband

Contraband is anything that is not permitted into the institution. This includes certain brands of shoes or sneakers, cell phones, drugs, alcohol, cigarettes, foods, etc. COs that bring these items into the jail are called mules.

Mules

COs sometimes have established a rapport with certain inmates. These inmates may be leaders among their peers or even drug dealers who have made a name for themselves and have enough money and connections to continue their operations from behind bars. In these instances, some COs are "on the take" or corrupt and may offer to bring in contraband (for a fee, of course), serving as a major contributor to the black market. Inmates often refer to these COs as "corruptions officers."

Some COs have a secret fascination with the way inmates interact, or maybe they are empathetic because a friend or family member is incarcerated. These COs might mule something in to set themselves apart from other COs and let select inmates know that they're willing to straddle the fence, although payment in these instances is not always required.

The Black Market

At the county level, the black market moves fast and sloppily. After all, most of the inmates participating were arrested for something similar, if not the same things they're attempting to obtain. For those who know how to operate the black market smoothly, the risk is worth the reward for the COs.

Why would COs put their jobs on the line? The answer is simple. Besides money, some of them honestly think that they know enough to continue to play both sides of the fence and not get caught. Others get sucked in.

When Mules Get Caught with Contraband

What happens when a CO gets caught?

There are numerous answers to this question because it depends on what stage in the game they get caught. For instance, when a CO gets caught red-handed with drugs, cell phones, or weapons, they face prosecution just like anyone else. If the contraband is something trivial like cigarettes in a non-smoking jail or tattoo ink, the administration might offer them an opportunity to save face by resigning.

When an Inmate Gets Caught with Contraband

If an inmate gets caught with drugs, alcohol, shanks, or cell phones, the inmate could actually receive new charges. If the contraband is not illegal but rather an infraction of institutional policy, the penalty can range from a verbal warning to a few weeks of cell restriction. These include items from the kitchen possibly used to manufacture jailhouse wine, articles of clothing that don't belong to the inmate, or even something as simple as having extra pillows, sheets, and pillowcases. These are examples of contraband that are not major and the penalty can range from a verbal warning to a few weeks of cell restriction.

Cell Restriction

Cell restriction is when you are confined to your cell 23 hours a day. However, you are still in your regularly assigned cell in the general population. You can still watch television in your cell or listen to your radio or Walkman, and your cellmates will still be allowed to come and go. You will also, more than likely, lose some privileges, such as commissary, phone calls, and block recreation.

The hour you are allowed receive to exercise and to shower (by yourself) once everyone is locked in.

The Hole

Most inmates will take cell restriction over "the hole," which is solitary confinement. But there are some who prefer the hole and are mentally conditioned to undergo that type of punishment.

An inmate who has no problem going into the hole is marked by administration as a problem. That's because the hole is designed to break the spirit of inmates and crush them mentally and socially.

But this tactic has been known to backfire. Not only will segregation allow you to take a look at yourself, but it also forces you to deal with your demons. I've seen guys go to the hole that was wild and uncivilized and come out entirely different individuals. Some find religion. Others find that the time alone is what they need to mature mentally. And some just simply got their priorities in order, learning from the mistakes that put them in the hole; they know that's not where they want to go again.

Inmates who refine themselves while they're in the hole are threats to the institution because they demonstrate the ability not only to adapt to the worse conditions of the jail but also to improve themselves while being there.

The New Jim Crow

People thought slavery had been abolished, but the prison system is a supporter of it. According to the 13th Amendment to the U.S. Constitution: "Neither slavery nor involuntary servitude, except as a punishment for crime whereof the party shall have been convicted, shall exist within the United States, or any place subject to their jurisdiction."

This means that individuals who take that oath to become COs are, in fact, vowing to be slave drivers. This gives an explanation as to why the highest pay to inmates is under $1 per day and the lowest pay is 18 cents, depending on the state in which you're incarcerated.

CHAPTER THREE

Bail and Bail Bondsmen

I couldn't possibly give you the full experience of jail without covering the bail and bond process and the anxieties that go along with it.

If the judge gives you a secured bail or a cash-only bail, the first thing you must do is figure out a way to come up with the money or collateral that you need to either pay the court or the bail bonds agent. A bail bonds service is an agency comprised of people who are in the business of bailing people out of jail. They have the finances, bonds, collateral, and rapport with the courts to get you released from prison while you await your court dates.

They usually get you out of jail for a portion of the amount you would have to pay if you had to pay for the bail directly. Sometimes they charge as little as 10 percent of whatever your bail actually is. Other times, it's higher depending on the charges. In most instances, they will accept collateral, such as the deed of your family member's or friend's home, a car title, or something to that effect. Their signatures and collateral heighten the chance that you'll appear in court and not flee because, if you decide to skip court, those who cosign for you could lose their property/collateral.

Bail Anxiety

The anxieties you will experience when trying to make bail can result in an emotional roller-coaster in itself. First of all, you have to find a bail bondsman that has reasonable prices. You can usually find a bail bonds agent in the telephone book or by references from other inmates or staff. And sometimes they are posted on the wall near telephones on the cell blocks.

If you do not have the means to make bail, you must attempt to come up with the required amount. This is where the reality of who you are, what you've done, and how your family members and friends view your character sets in.

If you have the financial means or collateral to post bail, then bailing out is just a matter of contacting the people who you trust enough to handle this responsibility for you. The key word is "trust" because I've seen plenty of instances where a person calls a family member or friend to retrieve money they had tucked away for a rainy day only to find out that the family member or friend decided to spend it.

If you have reliable people in your corner along with your own means to post bail, getting bailed out should be a problem for you. However, something from the past—from a traffic violation or a mix-up with your identity—could prevent you from being released even after bail is posted.

Some people don't even bother to call their folks or friends to try to make bail because they know they simply don't have the money. Some people attempt to call for bail, but they've burned their bridges and can't find anyone to help them. Others call home to a family member who has the means to bail them out, but they think it would be best if they stayed in jail and learned a lesson. Some call home for bail assistance only to hear promises and sob stories that turn into unintentional lies.

Some inmates opt to stay in jail and not even attempt to make bail because once they are released from jail on bail to await court dates, the time served stops. That means if you are convicted of the crime you've been accused of and have to return to prison, you don't receive credit for the time you were out. If you had stayed in jail and not bailed out, the time you had served would have been credited to your sentence, which would result in your getting out earlier. However, even if you know you'll probably be convicted or found guilty as charged, some people bail out anyway so that they can handle pre-sentencing business.

Pre-sentencing Business

Pre-sentencing business can include trying to get caught up with particular bills or obligations, preparing friends and loved ones for your incarceration, putting prized possessions or items in storage, or finding a good place to hide them while you're away. It may also entail selling property, such as cars, homes, etc., especially if you may be gone for a long time.

While the pre-sentencing business I've discussed above may appear like general tasks, they are not. Trying to prepare friends, family members and loved ones for your inevitable exit from their lives can really be a traumatic experience for everyone involved. And attempting to store something you consider invaluable or entrusting the responsibility of caring for it to someone while you are gone can prove daunting. And selling your home or car before you are sentenced can create anxieties, especially if you're unable to do so before you have to return to court.

I imagine the advantage for those who make bail would be that they are able to handle their pre-sentencing business. Another advantage is that they are able to have direct access to their lawyers, the Internet, and civilian law libraries. Making bail is a plus because it also enables you to have some time to enjoy life before you have to go to jail.

Lawyers and Public Defenders

If you can afford an attorney, s/he can do a professional job at keeping you informed on the particulars of your case either by visiting you at the jail, allowing you to call them collect or communication via correspondence.

However, unless you can afford a high-powered attorney or law firm, the lawyer you hire will probably be a local who is at the courthouse so much that she developed relationships with everyone there, including judges and district attorneys. And because you don't have any real financial means, the chances of your attorney going above and beyond the call of duty for you are slim to none!

On the other hand, if you cannot afford an attorney, "one will be appointed to you." That's part of your Miranda Rights. And that means the court will assign an attorney to your case. This attorney is called a public defender and is often referred by inmates as a public pretender. These court-appointed lawyers often have so many cases that it's common for them not even to know a client's name. And often, with public defenders, you can almost smell defeat before the battle has even begun.

Public defenders work for the state and their interest in you is not personal, by far. Their job is to give you the least amount of legal assistance. It's like having liability insurance on your vehicle versus full coverage. Many inmates that are represented by public defenders end up coping a plea agreement.

Lawyer Fees

Lawyers usually charge for the number of court hearings they attend with you and for you and also for submitting and filing paperwork, including motions and petitions. If you are versed in the law, you could actually file some of this paperwork yourself. But documents as important as these should be left up to a professional. You know what they say about a man who represents himself in court… "he has a fool for a client."

The fees usually increase as the case moves from arraignment and the preliminary hearing to case reviews, evidentiary and pre-trial hearings, the trial, sentencing and appeals.

Be aware of lawyers who give you a reasonably set fee but sell you out in the long run. And be mindful of those high-powered lawyers you thought you could afford initially until you learn how much they are requesting to continue representing you through trial.

Importance of Trial

The reason trial is so important and expensive is because this is where the lawyer must really perform. They have to convince the jury of your innocence, whereas, in the hearings leading up to trial, the attorneys can allow their staff to do most of the research and paperwork. All the lawyers have to do is show up at a hearing and speak a few words on your behalf to the District Attorney who is prosecuting your case.

Plea Agreements

The state wants a conviction. And when inmates can't afford to go to trial, they generally cop pleas to lesser charges and end up with much less time than if they went to trial and were found guilty of the crime of which they were accused.

A plea agreement is also referred to as "taking a deal" because the inmate feels content with the agreement and the state is satisfied with the conviction.

Sentencing

After the plea agreement or conviction at trial is the sentencing hearing. This is usually the final hearing unless you choose to appeal the outcome of your sentence. Let's say that you receive a sentence of 3 to 5 years. This means you must remain in jail for at least three years, but no more than five years. After you do at least three years, you will be eligible for parole.

However, if you have been getting into trouble and have several write-ups and infractions in your prison file, you can kiss an early parole release goodbye. When this happens, the person usually has to complete their entire sentence, so the thought of parole is an actual incentive to behave and stay under the radar.

County Sentence vs. State Sentence

Sentences more than one year long will be completed in a state prison. If your sentence is less than one year, you can and probably will do your time in the county jail. By the time you go through the entire court process, you may have done time anywhere from six to eight months in the county jail. However, if you have to do state time, the transition can be a bit tough, especially for first-timers.

When in county, you are most likely close to home and family and friends visit regularly. You also probably got to know a few people in county that you've become close with and, for survival reasons, have watched each other's back. The departure from that circle alone stirs up emotion.

Finally, the thought of going to a new jail where there are new people with new attitudes, problems and issues are difficult because of the X-factor—the unknown. State prison is far different from county jail, and the rumors that circulate throughout the county jail about the levels of intensity in state prison—the Big House—are vast!

Transfer to State Penitentiary

Your transfer to the state penitentiary can take anywhere from a few weeks to a few months, depending on the availability of bed space at the prison where you are being moved.

The bus ride to the state prison can be lengthy and being handcuffed and shackled to one or two people for long periods of time can be difficult. You may get lucky and get shipped to a prison only an hour or two away from your home, or you may end up in a prison on the other side of the state.

Welcome to the Big House

As soon as you arrive, you'll understand why they call it the Big House. Most penitentiaries are as large as a college campus and designed similarly. However, instead of fraternity buildings and dormitories, you have housing units and cell blocks. Instead of green grass to lie down on to relax and study, you have a big prison yard with dumbbells and weight pits. Both are equipped with fields for sporting events such as softball, football (flag), soccer and outside basketball courts.

Most big houses can also have separate buildings, including dining/chow halls, education/trade buildings, gymnasiums, and administration buildings.

Now let's go inside.

Once you step off the bus, you'll most likely get a quick verbal rundown from one of the state correctional officers about how you're no longer in a county jail, along with a brief summary of the rules, regulations, and the conduct expected during your stay at that prison. Then you'll be escorted into the receiving area, where you'll be placed into holding tanks.

Holding Tanks

These holding tanks are more civilized than the ones at the county jail or police precinct, where you were taken after your arrest. That's because, by the time you get to the state penitentiary, you're pretty much cleaned up from any serious drug addictions or withdrawals, and the mentally ill have been classified into separate units, so you don't have to worry about sharing the tank with them. And the unfortunate homeless individuals who were fresh off the street in the precinct and county holding tanks are now showered, rested, and well-fed.

For the most part, in the holding tank stage, everyone exists on the same plane and finds a way to get along.

Get in Where You Fit in

Once you are classified to go into the general population and find out what housing unit/block you will be living on, you will have no choice but to get in where you fit in. This is where it all happens: gangs, religious groups, and athletes all sizing you up, looking at the new recruit from the first step you take into the general population. The physique of some of these inmates will let you know that you're in a different world—and you are!

Convict vs. Inmate

You may often hear people interchange convict and inmate. But a convict is a person who has actually been convicted of their crime and is serving the sentence. Therefore, I will use the word convict or prisoner instead of inmate because if you're in the state prison, you've obviously been convicted of the crime you've been accused of committing.

Last Stop

For some, state prison is the last stop. It's the end of your road, literally. You will never be on another road or take another ride again. That's because you've either been sentenced to life or death or received so many years that you'll die before completing your sentence. Or you may receive a short-term sentence but end up committing a capital or more serious offense, which requires that you remain in state prison until the sun burns out.

This is one of many reasons why you can become a permanent prisoner.

Tattoos

The state prison system is similar to the county jail but magnified by 10, including the mentality of the prisoners and COs. For instance, in the county, you can get tattoos from some of your fellow inmates even though they will be from homemade ink and probably hand-plucked with a homemade tattooing needle.

In the state, you can get more professional-looking tattoos, which will be done by guys with much more experience and better equipment. Specifically, the tattooing gun will be electric or battery-operated. While it will still be homemade, the equipment is equivalent to professional manufacturers'. The needles will be shaved from guitar strings and/or sewing kits, and the ink will be genuine tattoo ink (smuggled in by a mule).

Homosexual Activity

In county, you may witness a few experiences of homosexual activity. In state prison, some men who had never had sexual experiences with men before may become involved in homosexual activity. That's because, after so many years of not having an intimate relationship with women, they fall victim to their hormones.

In state prison, men marry men. Others have been raped so often they end up adopting the lifestyle. Some were gay when they arrived and being honest about their lifestyle gets them respect. And some we call closet queens; a closet queen acts tough in the yard and pretends to be homophobic, but in every opportunity he finds, he indulges in the act behind closed doors. His motto is similar to Las Vegas: "What's done in jail stays in jail!"

But don't think that convicts who indulge in homosexual activity are soft. In fact, most are tough with iron pumped physiques and they have learned to defend themselves against predators and vicious attacks.

Importance of Visits

Nothing helps you through your sentence more than the support of family and friends. Visits indicate exactly how many people are in your corner. And except for unforeseen or uncontrollable circumstances, the people who visit you are the people who are concerned about you the most. Now that's not to say that everyone who doesn't visit you doesn't care about or love you. It's just that when you're out of sight, you're out of their minds.

If you didn't receive many visits at the county level during your incarceration, you can almost bank on the fact that you'll receive even fewer when you get to state prison.

If you're still getting visits by the time you're transferred to the state penitentiary, your support team is pretty genuine. That's because a lot of the time, people hang around while you're going through the court proceedings to see if you're going to win your case and get released. Once they find out you've been convicted and sentenced, they figure you're not going anywhere for a while, so they take a different approach on visiting.

As far as family and true friends go, it's not that they love you any less because you are now officially doing time. It's that life must still go on for them and they must adapt to your absence.

However, there are a number of factors that can contribute to the amount of visits you receive. First, it depends on where you end up in the state system. If you are in a prison several hours away from your home, transportation alone can play a significant role in the amount of visits you receive, if any. Also, some families don't have the financial means for travel and some can't afford to miss the time away from work.

Relationships While in Prison

The fewer contacts you have with the outside world, the easier it is for relationships to end, especially those that were not built on solid ground. With a lack of visits and a minimal amount of phone calls, it is very easy for your significant other (if you had one) to give in to the temptations that exist in the free world. That means beginning to live out the newfound desires of her heart and leaving you while you're locked up.

Although this is a common occurrence, there are plenty of Winnie Mandela's out there who are more than capable of withstanding the test of time.

However, when a marriage or relationship is destroyed because of the effects of prison life, it can impact you in many different ways. For one, the mental and emotional time and commitment that the convict was putting into the relationship can now be withdrawn and the convict now has that much more space in their lives to work on their own problems, flaws and issues. This can definitely be a plus if viewed from this perspective. On the other hand, everyone doesn't always view things optimistically, and a breakup while locked up can be viewed as inconsiderate and cowardly and incite bitter feelings within the convict.

CHAPTER FOUR

Being Happy in Prison

There is a barrage of feelings that convicts experience, both negative and positive, and different ways they choose to deal with them. You might wonder how you can be happy in prison. There are a variety of things that can make a convict happy while in prison. Believe it or not, some people are actually happy that they are in prison.

Drug users who were really far gone in their addiction may be happy to be in prison. Prison gives them a reprieve from running the streets and indulging in drugs. It gives their minds and bodies the rest they need. Some say prison rescued them. Nothing like time in prison to pump iron, read books, get rest, eat free meals, and never have to be concerned with debt.

Good news can also bring convicts happiness. Of course, it can make anyone anywhere happy, but in prison, where spirits are so easily crushed, good news can offer happiness where there is no other means or remedy.

Being Sad in Prison

While "sadness" is a feeling I don't have to expound on too

much, there are a few things that can make a prisoner especially sad. Being away from home is chief.

There are certain things or events that take place that can cause you sadness, such as a song playing on the radio that reminds you of a particular time, place, or relationship. Reminiscing alone can trigger sadness. But when you combine it with a familiar tune on the radio, you have the perfect recipe for sadness.

The holidays and birthdays are also a real doozie, especially for first timers and short timers. Most guys that have been in for a while or plan on being in for a long time have become numb to the holidays and birthdays. In prison, your birthday is nothing special. As a matter of fact, every convict has a birthday almost every day, so there's nothing significant about yours. This fact brings about sadness.

Luck/Fortune

Luck is a common feeling among short-timers. For the short-timer, just knowing you'll be released in a few years is good reason to feel fortunate, especially when you can see others around you with extremely lengthy and life sentences. The thought that things could have been much worse never leaves your mind as you look into the eyes of long-timers day in and day out.

Others feel fortunate with the outcome of their court cases and the opportunities that will exist after their short-term incarceration. Newcomers and first-timers are also fortunate when they make it through the system without too much hassle. They are lucky to be able to adapt to things despite the vicious stories they've heard prior to going to prison.

Anger and Resentment

Although there are anger management groups, classes and programs in prison, they are often watered-down and serve more as sessions for venting rather than for learning how to manage anger.

On the other hand, there are those who are angry to the bitter end. They don't need to have a reason. Although they have far shorter sentences than others, they feel as though they've been dealt a bad hand or have received a raw deal. Some have a hard time adapting or adjusting to prison life.

The majority of prisoners claim to be innocent, but some of them actually are. If you put yourself in their shoes, what would you do if you were actually innocent of a crime but are convicted of it and serving time? This type of injustice happens all the time all across the United States. Although the criminal justice system is well structured, there are still many flaws in it. So, when an innocent person is incarcerated, they have a right to be angry.

Although all feelings are valid because everyone is entitled to their personal opinions, there are those who think life owes them something. And they are angry because they do not feel as though they've received whatever it is they deserve. They wear anger on their sleeves either because that is the only way they know how to deal with it or because that's the way in which they choose to deal with it.

Anger is a common emotion that's experienced by almost everyone in prison at one time or another, but it's the lack of control or the absence of knowing how to control the anger that leads to altercations, problems and complications.

Joyfulness

Believe it or not, inmates and convicts have moments of joyfulness. A good visit or phone call with family or friends is enough to give one the feeling of joyfulness for several weeks or even months. Of course, it all depends on how often you get to receive visits or make phone calls.

The thought of being in an uncivilized environment around hardened convicts all day, every day and never being able to let your guard down can easily keep you on edge. To have the opportunity to escape the madness, even for just a few hours during a visit with your family and friends, and to get hugs and kisses and receive news from home can bring the convict feelings of joyfulness.

Anxiety

Anxiety is another feeling that prisoners experience. Waiting on mail, phone calls, visits, a decision from the Parole Board and many other things will contribute to a prisoner's anxieties.

It can be something as simple as lunch didn't fill you up and, because you can't have seconds, you anxiously await dinner. Or it can be as complex as you're down to the last 30 days of your sentence and it seems as if time is moving slower than ever.

Disappointment

Some of the disappointments prisoners experience come in the form of a missed visit, an unanswered phone call, or a delayed money order needed for commissary. But the Parole Board is one of the best examples to use.

Many prisoners participate in all the groups and programs the prison has to offer. They remain free of write-ups and infractions but are still refused parole. No matter how prisoners conduct themselves in a model fashion and abide by all the rules and regulations, they still don't make parole. Why?

Acceptance, Accountability, Remorse and Reform

Accepting responsibility for your crime is an indicator that you are taking accountability for your action. Through all of this, remorse often surfaces. And once a convict begins to feel remorseful for their crime and actions, their heart will soften and that will increase the chances of their reform. It all begins with acceptance.

Denial and Dishonesty

When prisoners are in denial of their crime or actions, it will be that much more difficult for them to become reformed. Denial can exist on many levels for many different reasons. Some people are simply dishonest, regardless to whom or what. Some people have been telling lies for so long, they don't know how to tell the truth. Although it would seem that everyone should know right from wrong, that's not always the case. Some people were born into crime, lies and dishonesty. Some people don't have common sense.

Unfortunately, these types of people make up a large percentage of the criminals that re-offend or violate their probation and/or parole. When a prisoner is accepting, you know they're on the pathway to reform.

Sorrow, Regret and Remorse

Just because you feel sorrow doesn't necessarily mean you're feeling it for the right reasons. Some convicts are sorry that they got caught. They regret not having been better at pulling off their crime.

On the contrary, some convicts are, in fact, sorry for what they did and they do regret their actions. They wish they could turn back the hands of time so that they could have made much better decisions and exercised better judgment on the days leading up to their offense.

During parole hearings, having remorse, regret and sorrow for the crimes you commit can increase your chances of making parole, especially if all parties deem these feelings to be genuine. Otherwise, remorse, regret, and sorrow are feelings that will ultimately contribute to refining your character.

Individuals who are secure with themselves have little or no problem feeling sorrow or regret. Others are just too hardened and tough to ever allow those types of feelings to enter their being.

Thankful and Grateful

Convicts can feel thankful and grateful for the smallest things. Things that people in the free world take for granted, someone who is incarcerated will appreciate it ten times over.

For example, a convict is issued one or two rolls of toilet paper per week, and this supply is supposed to last for the entire week. But in prison, toilet paper has more than one use. It's used as tissue to blow your nose and doubles as paper towels, dusting cloths, and napkins.

In state institutions, prisoners are fed low-grade food. Consequently, nausea and diarrhea are the norm. But what happens when prisoners run out of toilet paper before the end of the week? They will have to try to hustle up another roll from a fellow prisoner and if that's not possible, the alternative is ripping up a sheet or T-shirt to serve that purpose.

Another thing prisoners are grateful for are gifts of money they receive from their family and friends. Mental and emotional support can keep your spirits up as well, but financial support from home is incomparable! Money orders sent by your family and friends are credited to your account and can be spent in the commissary store.

Then there are those prisoners who just count their blessings every day. They're thankful for the fundamental things, like food, clothing, shelter and good health. They're thankful because God woke them up to see another day and the burden that was placed on them was not too much to bear.

Distress

Prisoners can also feel distressed for various reasons. For one, being away from your home and loved ones, especially if you're having a difficult time accepting your present reality, which is prison. On a similar note, prisoners can experience distress when they call home and there is no answer.

A lack of understanding about your situation can bring on

distress as well. Even when civilians go into a situation in the blind, the thought of the unknown alone can cause distress; imagine a prisoner's distress about being in limbo concerning a court case, appeal, or parole decision.

People often say: "Don't worry about things you can't change or things you have no control over." But I'll be the first to tell you, in prison, that is so much easier said than done. Doing time is just that, it's time. You have nothing but time and after enough time locked in your cell, it's very common for the walls to start closing in on you and for your mind to begin playing tricks on you. You have nothing but time to worry about every little thing and over analyze situations that a person who was not incarcerated would have possibly gotten over or forgotten.

Unless you're just a worry-wart or are prone to stress, feelings of distress will eventually wear off once you learn to accept your environment.

Reassurance and Confirmation

For prisoners, there is nothing like the feeling of reassurance or receiving confirmation of a situation.

Confirmation and reassurance are extremely important in prison because prison is a place where trust gets broken and dreams are shattered. Real-life events can prevent family and friends from keeping their word. Consider that you're expecting a visit at the end of the month from a member of your family or a friend, which provides you with positive energy and inspiration. And as the days grow closer to the planned visit, your anxiety naturally heightens. To alleviate some of that anxiety, you call home to make sure that everything is going as scheduled and you receive confirmation that they will be there. That type of reassurance is what turns anxiety into excitement.

Other examples include knowing a bail has been posted, your case is back in court on appeal and you have a good chance of getting it overturned, you've made parole and have a confirmed release date, and that things are fine on the home front.

Loneliness and Abandonment

Feelings of loneliness in prison can cause you to become open or vulnerable to people or things that might come your way. In an attempt to fill that void, you might unknowingly invite or attract predators who await the opportunity to infiltrate the lonely fellow prisoner.

Religion in Prison

There are several religions practiced in prison. The most popular religions are Islam, Christianity, Catholicism, and Jehovah's Witnesses.

Although there are many prisoners who leave religion behind in prison when they return home, there are many others who continue to practice their newfound religion. Practicing religion can lead to becoming an upstanding, law-abiding citizen. When you have a religious foundation, it serves to provide for the success of a lot of prominent people, and prisoners are not exempt.

Religion also gives prisoners something positive to focus on and to study, plus, it is a good way to meet good fellow prisoners who aren't indulging in negative behavior.

Practicing religion is an excellent way to utilize your time in prison. I know that doesn't sound to righteous, but it's important to get through the days, weeks, months and years you spend there. But most importantly, religion is important for the spirit. The human being is comprised of three dimensions: mind, body, and soul. Religion is imperative to feed the spirit versus leaving the spirit to remain dormant.

CHAPTER FIVE

Behavior

An individual's personality, thoughts, and attitude generally determines their behavior. Combine these elements with uncontrolled emotions and instability and you have a mix that you shouldn't take lightly.

Any day, anywhere, at any time—24 hours a day, 7 days a week, 365 days a year—you can either witness or become part of the savage and inhumane side of fellow prisoners, disgruntled COs or staff. Just because people have been locked away for a significant period of time, or just because COs and staff oversee prisoners, doesn't mean they have appropriate training.

With any possible number of situations that can happen to prisoners, it's almost the norm for them to lash out in anger or to become aggressive. But this type of behavior most certainly spells trouble, the kind of trouble that can result in plenty of paperwork, blood, sweat, and tears and possibly even death.

Does everyone react negatively to tough, emotional situations or intense prison tribulations? Of course not! There are plenty of prisoners standing firmly on a foundation of positivity, but they, too, can become deadly if you force their hand.

Survival

Prison is all about survival, which means mental, physical, and spiritual survival!

Although physical and mental survival goes hand-in-hand, it is not mandatory that your mind and body be equally strong to survive a prison sentence. Me personally, I'll take brains over brawn any day! Because with good decision-making skills, you can elude physical confrontation throughout your entire prison stay. Another reason I'll pick brains over brawn is because administration is notorious for playing mind games and those who are not of a strong, sound mind will have an extremely hard time surviving.

Mental Survival

Mental survival could be, in fact, the most important of all because all thoughts and decisions take place in the mind first, long before they ever turn into action, behavior, or habit.

If your mind is not strong, lacks focus, or is easily influenced, you may not be up to the task of sending out the best possible survival signals to the rest of your body. You see this often with mentally ill patients. Although they find some kind of way to cope, there's a big difference between your mind staying on auto-pilot and kicking your survival mechanisms into as needed versus just getting by mode.

Remember the saying, "Only the strong survive?" I'm almost certain the average person interprets this saying as only physical and/or mental. Well, survival encompasses three components. Some guys get shipped to state prison as young as 18 years of age and, by no fault of their own (just a lack of maturity and knowledge), their behavior reflects their mental capacity, which is underdeveloped and juvenile.

Then you have some of the older guys who just can't seem to break their adolescent mentality, either because they've been incarcerated since they were juveniles and just can't seem to make the mental transition or because they feel comfortable playing around and goofing off.

Remember I told you that there are many different ways that prisoners get through their sentences. Believe it or not, some people actually choose to clown around the whole time. You can almost be certain they'll reoffend because they never got the gist of their punishment.

It's common for convicts that are not that mentally adept (but do have potential) to get drafted and schooled by those who are sharper. This contributes to the mental makeovers that are often needed to draw up strategies. After all, you are in a different world now, away from society, so it's only logical that your thoughts and views change to adapt to your new environment.

Now, on the other hand, convicts that are not mentally sharp and have little or no potential for refinement or upgrade tend to fall into a category of weaker class prisoners. We all know what happens to weak people or weak-minded people—they are taken advantage of.

If your mind is not already sharp and on point, then my suggestion would be that you should immediately learn to condition your mind to prepare it for survival in your new world.

A big part of mental survival is having excellent awareness (notice that I didn't say have a good awareness or great awareness). You actually need excellent awareness to heighten your chances of survival in prison. You should know everything that's going on around you at all times whether it's your business or not. There's a huge difference between knowing everything that's going on around you and minding other people's business. Just because you know things doesn't mean you have to act on them or even lead on like you know anything. It's just your personal duty to be aware. Minding other people's business is a no-no because what's done in jail is supposed to stay in jail; that's an unwritten code. Some of the things people are involved in could get them into serious trouble with administration or get them hurt by some of the other prisoners. Even worse, they can be killed because integrity was on the line and information was leaked. So, of course, always mind your own business.

Here are a few examples as to why it would be in your best interest to be aware of everything that's going on around you, even the smallest things.

Let's say that your cellmate is mixed up in gambling (for the record, I picked gambling out of the blue). He gambles every day as part of his daily routine and pastime. Gambling in jail is similar to black market street gambling, but the difference is that if you come up short when payment is due, you have no place to run. Of course, you can always check into Protective Custody, but that would immediately tarnish your reputation among your peers. Not only that, before administration places you under that type of custody, they are going to probe into why you need protection and what you need protection from.

Without the money or collateral to cover your debt, one or more prisoners can seek physical retribution and possibly even be armed with homemade jailhouse weapons. Although physical attacks can be carried out anywhere within the institution, it's common for convicts to fight inside the cells in an attempt to be discrete.

Consequently, if you happen to be present when the attack is going down, you too could be seriously injured or killed, or you could be accused of conspiracy in the incident. How could you have avoided all of this? By having heightened awareness. Excellent awareness brings about foresight and foresight brings about survival.

You need to be aware of who you are dealing with or involved with on any level. Knowing someone who is at the prison with you prior to coming to prison is not enough reason to warrant immediate trust. A lot of prisoners have vicious skeletons in their closets, so you really need to do some investigating and observing of your own instead of taking anything for granted or at face value.

If you are not careful and watchful and don't screen your acquaintances, you are setting yourself up to get caught up in whatever they are involved in, either by manipulation, voluntarily, or by plain ole obliviousness.

Imagine a so-called buddy asking you to hold something for him. It could be clothes, shoes, cigarettes or groceries. The reason why a prisoner would want another prisoner to hold items for him is because the rules have a cap on how many items one prisoner is entitled to possess.

Now, if someone asks you to hold an item for him, and you decide to hold that item either on your person or in your cell, your antenna needs to go up; that's a red flag.

Your awareness should kick right in and first, ask your buddy if the item is or contains contraband. Next, you should thoroughly check the items yourself. Remember, contraband is having something that's not supposed to be in your possession, even extra commissary items.

If you don't inspect the items for yourself and, for whatever reason, the COs decide to do a random cell or body search and you are in possession of the contraband, guess who's going to bite that bullet? And you'd better hope that it is the type of trouble that can be resolved in-house and not deliberated at the courthouse.

Physical Survival

On the flip side, convicts who tend to work out and stay physically fit can easily deter predators from even thinking about making an attempt of a violent nature.

There's entirely too much testosterone in a male prison for things not to get physical every day, whether it's on the basketball court, at the card table, during meals or any place else you can think of. This is one of the reasons why convicts who are small in size and stature often go above and beyond to pump iron and get on some kind of intense workout regime. They want to beef up their frame and maximize their strength.

But don't get it confused. Size doesn't always matter because even a dwarf can stab you with a homemade weapon, or split your head open with one of the loose dumbbells from the weight pile. You know what they say: "The bigger they are, the harder they fall."

Spiritual Survival

Spiritual strength creates a balance within, but your spirit is where your *will* resides. And, where there's a *will,* there's a way. This could make all the difference in survival.

There are numerous ways to feed the spirit. Some do it through religion and some do it through meditation. Some do it by surrounding themselves with positive people and maintaining an optimistic outlook. And some people feed their spirit in ways I can't even imagine, but it works for them and gets them by.

Many people (not only prisoners) are not even aware that they have a spirit. Even those who are aware do not feed it and it lies dormant. Some people are too wicked to have any kind of positive, godly spirit dwell in them, so they are possessed and consumed by evil spirits and demons.

The reality of it is spending time nurturing your spirit can keep you away from a lot of elements that you don't need to be around in the first place, ultimately keeping you out of harm's way.

If you are one of the unfortunate ones who is possessed by evil spirits and demons, then my suggestion to you is to keep your views to yourself and other like-minded people. That's because in prison you must be very careful about what you ask for because you will get what you're looking for.

Psychological Medication

There is one alternative that prisoners exercise when prison has mentally consumed them and they just can't cope. They sign up for psychological medication. The process is too easy. All they have to do is make an appointment to see the prison psychologist who will ask a few questions and run some generic tests. Sometimes the prison will encourage weak-minded prisoners to take medication in a genuine attempt to help the prisoner adjust or cope. Other times, they're just creating Guinea pigs. Some prisoners on these medications look like they're zombies and don't know whether they're coming or going. And those with mental health issues are medicated to the point that they've had any spirit knocked right out of them. It's like they're the real walking dead.

Developing Habits/Rituals

It's very common for men and women to come to prison and pick up habits and rituals they did not have or practice before they arrived, including religion, good hygiene, reading, education—and the list goes on.

Respect is another positive habit or character trait some convicts learn in prison. Respect will take you a very long way, not only in prison but also in life. In most cases, when you give respect, you get respect. Unfortunately, sometimes in prison, you have to demand respect.

Negative Habits and/or Traits You Pick Up in Prison

Some of the negative habits or traits that people in prison pick up include taking medications and smoking cigarettes. Having a smoking habit is not only bad for your health, but in prison, it's even more detrimental. For instance, if your cellmate doesn't smoke, you will be polluting his air, which is an easy way to end up in an altercation. Another reason smoking is a negative habit in prison is if you're not rich or well off, cigarettes are very expensive.

Another bad habit is those who are weak, lonely and vulnerable seek friendship in the wrong places with the wrong people and fall victim to homosexuality. Prison does not provide adequate protection for sexual encounters and disease is easily spread. That's how some prisoners bring something home to their loved ones or even die during incarceration.

Finally, others start using illegal drugs in prison, even those who had never used before. This is unfortunate because sometimes, getting off drugs is not as easy as getting on them. And this could lead to a painful, possibly harmful withdrawal or other side effects.

A few things can go wrong when you're involved in narcotics in prison. For instance, possession is nine-tenths of the law, meaning that if you get caught with drugs while you're in prison, you're in for some serious trouble. You can expect to be arrested and charged just as if you are in the free world, plus you'll also probably have some in-house offenses and repercussions to deal with. This is a very easy way to get time added on to your sentence. Unfortunately, this is a common event in prisons all across America.

You might ask, "Why would people knowingly want to compound their problems?" I have two answers: (1) they are not the best thinkers or decision makers, and; (2) some people just enjoy living on the edge.

Some of the in-house repercussions I am referring to as violations of this sort would most likely consist of some serious time in solitary confinement. Individuals will also most likely be shipped out of that prison to another prison because dealing drugs in prison are considered disrupting the normal operation of the prison and breaching security, not to mention the mark that will be permanently attached to your name throughout your entire prison stay.

Even if administration did a random urine screen that came back positive, you would still face the above repercussions. The difference is there won't be any formal charges filed; everything would probably be handled in-house. But you can kiss parole or an early release goodbye!

Another question would be: *Is it worth it?*

Earlier in the book, I mentioned how some people are very

comfortable in prison than when they are confronted with these types of situations, it's no big deal because they know what it was and every detail involved before they even participated. Others were clueless as to the realm of possibilities that existed and were forced into learning the hard way. Prison certainly is the school of hard knocks.

CHAPTER SIX

101 Things

What are the 101 things you should know about jail?

1.   Once you're convicted of a crime, you have what's known as a criminal record. This means there's been a recording of your conviction, which is placed in the criminal justice system attached to your name, like a social security number or birth date. This record can be compared to a bad credit rating, except unlike a bad credit rating that can be removed after seven years, your criminal history is generally there for life unless you're a rare case where you can get it expunged. If you are convicted of a felony, you lose your right to bear arms. And in some states, you forfeit your voting privileges and depending on your crime, you could lose your driver's license. Criminal records could also hinder your credit, housing, and employment opportunities. However, there are still many programs and agencies that cater to individuals with a criminal record. There are programs where employers receive tax credits when they hire convicts, such as the Work Opportunities Tax Credit and the Federal Bonding Program (FBP). The Federal Bonding Program provides the employer with a special fidelity

bond for 12 months, free of charge, which protects the employer against any employee theft or dishonesty. The success rate of the FBP is 98.5 percent, which means that less than two percent of the bondees default on the bonds. For more information on these programs and others like them, contact your local job center or search the web.

2. Don't discuss your personal business in jail unless you've really connected with someone and developed and established trust. There are so many people with hidden agendas the possibilities are endless concerning what someone will do or say about your personal business.

3. Never introduce other inmates and convicts to your family. This is something that happens every day in prisons. Guys get lonely and they want to meet a new friend or pen pal. Trust me, let them work that kink out of their life on their own.

4. If you're not already one, become an excellent observer.

You can learn a lot about folks by watching, looking and listening.

5. Always remember the Golden Rule: "What's done in jail stays in jail." There's no need to bring the stories you hear or behaviors you experience back home with you. They only

contaminate your loved ones and neighbors.

6. Discipline yourself because there are a lot of things that will certainly tempt you. But remember: Everything that glitters ain't gold!

7. Try to maintain a good rapport with your family and true friends because they will probably be your strongest allies and support while you are incarcerated.

8. Choose your battles wisely! Know that every fight is not a good fight. They say a good run is better than a bad stance any day.

9. Remember, only the strong survive. Never show fear.

Don't be timid or cowardly. Don't expose your weaknesses.

10. Try your best to be a leader, not a follower, even if that means becoming a loner. If it's a must that you follow, be careful who and what it is you are following.

a. If you've made it to the penitentiary in the general population, you are obviously 18 years of age or older. At this age, you should not fall victim to peer pressure. In jail, someone could pressure you into a situation that can easily go from bad to worse or even HOPELESS!

11. Try to stay out of the way. Stay under the radar. The center

of attraction can result in becoming the center of attack.

12. All telephone calls and mail that is received are monitored. Also, your outgoing mail can be monitored if the administration places you under investigation for any reason.

13. Lending and borrowing is the way the economy runs on the black market in prison. But you should be extra careful not to indulge in the trading game because, for one, it's against the rules and regulations to lend or borrow anything from another prisoner. And if you can't pay your debts, there are several ways to deal with that and none of them are pretty.

14. Never snitch on someone. It scars your name during your entire prison term and you will always have to look over your shoulder.

15. Always mind your own business!

16. If you must be slick, it's your duty not to get caught. But remember it's the job of the staff to catch you.

17. There's nothing wrong with asking questions. If you don't know something, it's better to ask questions than to just stumble around in the blind—you might run into something you weren't trying to encounter!

18. Try to be empathetic to others. This could possibly prevent you from saying or doing the wrong things around the wrong people. Ultimately, being empathetic in prison can lessen your chances of unnecessary incidents and problems.

19. Don't look for friends! If you meet someone that you have some things in common with, let the relationship manifest itself naturally. Prison has nothing but prisoners and you never know when someone is running the con game on you.

20. Don't wear your emotions on your sleeve. That leaves you exposed and vulnerable to predators who would otherwise have passed you by if you weren't so emotionally advertised.

21. Don't be too prideful. If you're the type with too much pride, try to learn to be humble because pride can produce false courage, and false courage can make you act without thinking a situation all the way through.

22. Develop a daily routine or schedule. This not only makes the time go by faster but it also helps you get organized and being organized is an excellent trait to take home with you once you're released from prison.

23. Be careful when you get homemade, unprofessional tattoos

in prison. Although a lot of guys who create tattoos are skilled and do high-quality work, the homemade equipment is often recycled and not properly sterilized. This is one of the most common ways to contract diseases, including HIV, AIDS, and hepatitis.

24. Get a job. Not only will you earn a few extra dollars each month, but it will give you something positive to do to occupy your time. In some states, they even knock off a couple of days each month from your sentence if you work while incarcerated.

25. Don't have unrealistic expectations. This can really hold you back mentally because the intensity of expectation can be powerful and the reality of letdown can be even more devastating.

26. If you have the ability to read and write, take advantage of the prison library and law library. While everyone has their own preferences concerning what they like to read, I would advise reading material that increases your knowledge and educates you. Read the correct things. Always remember the more you know, the more you can do.

27. If you don't have a GED or high school diploma, sign up for classes immediately when you first arrive to prison. After all, what better time to achieve such an important goal.

28. The penitentiary also has vocational and trade classes that are only available to those who have a high school diploma or a GED.

29. There will be many distractions in prison, but it's important that you stay focused on the things that mean the most to you.

30. Take advantage of the treatment programs, such as Alcohol Anonymous, Narcotics Anonymous, violence prevention, and other therapeutic groups. Even though the programs are not the best, if you're sincere, you can still gain some good knowledge from them.

31. Do some serious soul searching until you arrive at your core issues. That way, you know what things you need to work on or correct, and you can formulate your plan of action accordingly.

32. Don't waste time because you can never get time back once it's gone. If you find yourself bored with nothing to do, write a letter, read a book, or exercise. But always stay busy.

33. Learn all of the policies, rules and regulations that govern the institution in which you are housed. It would be to your advantage to know them.

34. If you have a discrepancy with a staff member or a

legitimate claim where a policy has been violated and the results impact you, you need to learn the grievance system.

35. Expect change. Learn how to deal with change. Life is one big transition after another in an environment like prison, and change is the norm. A lot of the time, the administration will put a monkey wrench in the game just to throw the prisoners off from studying security patterns.

36. Be wary of jailhouse lawyers. Most of them are old heads serving long sentences, and while they do know a lot about the law and the way the court system works, they are hustlers. They can't get themselves out of prison, but for the right fee, they'll sell young, naïve prisoners the dream that they can get them out.

37. Cigarettes and postage stamps are considered currency in prison. This is what you'll need to do trading in the black market or to participate in gambling.

38. Sports are very big in jail. There are sporting activities to participate in within prison, such as softball, basketball, volleyball, handball, weightlifting, and horseshoes. Prisoners are also very interested in TV sports, no matter the season.

39. Soap operas are also very big in jail, especially in those

institutions that allow the prisoners to buy televisions for their cells.

40. If you are lonely and you need a companion, see if one of your friends or family members will create a web page for you or a social media site like MySpace or Facebook. This is an excellent way to meet new people.

41. Connect with pen pal services. This is not only a wonderful pastime, but you get to meet some interesting people who could possibly be helpful in your future.

42. There are organizations and prison advocacy groups that are designed to help prisoners and their families. These organizations provide an array of programs, ranging from moral support to transportation. Check your phone book or search the web under "prison" or "prisoner advocacy" in your city or state.

43. There are several buses, shuttles, and van services that will transport family and friends to prisons. Check your phonebook and on the Internet for local listings or call the prison where your loved one is housed for recommendations.

44. There are re-entry programs for former offenders designed specifically to assist with job training, job placement and other

relevant services. Reentry programs are often a plus for individuals with minimal support or no support system at all. Check the prison library or phonebook, ask other prisoners, or search the web if you have access. Every now and then, your prison counselor might know of a good reentry program.

45. The recidivism rate is absurd! During the time in which this book was compiled, an accurate statistic could not be assessed; however, an educated guess is over 60% of convicts who are released from prison re-offend. Some don't even last a week in society.

46. A prisoner is often treated less than a second-class citizen. Behind bars, respect is often lost between the prisoner, officers and administration. If this leads to incidents, it could result in cruel and unusual punishment by a CO, such as beating, not feeding, extending time in the hole, etc. Most times, these situations are covered up and the prisoner's voice is rarely heard. And even when it is heard, no one of importance will support the prisoner.

47. If you're the type of convict who has solid family support, they might also be subjected to negative treatment by COs.

48. Corrections Officers have their own little clicks within the

facility, they're not all united.

49. If your family provides you with your only source of income, then they are in for an economical surprise. Groceries at the prison commissary are marked up as high as three times the price you would pay for the item in society. Phone calls can cost up to five times the amount you would pay in the free world.

50. Board games are sold in the commissary. They are also handed out by the administration's Activities Department to be used in each unit. These games are supposed to help pass time, but they are actually pacifiers designed to keep prisoners focused on mediocre things.

51. Both prisoners and COs play mind games. That's why it's so important for you to get your mind right if it's not already.

52. Watch out for manufactured personalities. Prisoners tend to live out their alter ego, especially younger prisoners.

53. Jail is full of prisoners who are reformed and have genuinely good hearts.

54. Although jail has plenty of good and reformed prisoners, there are plenty of frauds, con artists and habitual liars as well.

55. Never underestimate anyone, even a lame can hurt,

maim or kill you.

56. Nothing is for free in the penitentiary. Generally, if someone gives you something, you can believe they have a hidden agenda.

57. Too much socialization can lead to a confrontation. In other words, don't become Mr. Joe Familiar.

58. Some people believe if you sleep 12 hours a day, you'll actually be serving only half of your sentence. However, this is one of the biggest myths of all because if you're sleeping half of the day away, you're wasting precious time that you could use more constructively.

59. When some people come to jail, they are in a serious relationship or are married. Due to the conditions of incarceration and the limits that have been placed between you, the partners/spouses opt to exit out of the relationship (either temporarily or permanently) and continue on with their lives.

60. Jail is not tense and serious every day. You have ups and downs.

61. Don't let the time do you! You do the time. What this basically means is don't let the time affect you in a negative way.

Try to stay in control of your actions and decisions.

62. Try your best not to bring unnecessary problems on yourself. You have enough problems on your hands dealing with the unknown experiences that await you throughout the course of the normal prison day.

63. Although most prisoners are adults, they all have different levels of education. This makes for a unique mental melting pot.

64. Usually, when someone gives you their word, it is supposed to be bond. Not in prison. Some prisoners live and die by their word, but others have a word that's about as solid as applesauce.

65. There are some COs who don't have an honest bone in their body. They will provoke situations with prisoners, write them up and then lie on the entire report.

66. Some prisoners join religious groups for the wrong reasons. They are seeking the unity and protection of the brotherhood instead of seeking God.

67. In state prison, the amount of time you're serving has no bearing on who you will be housed with. You could be serving a four-year sentence with a cellmate who is doing life.

68. Remember to always screen potential associates. One of your best defenses against bad intentions is foresight. Screening potential associates could assist you with who you'll be dealing with in the future.

69. Don't spread yourself too thin. Don't commit to too many people or things. Always leave yourself enough room for a way out.

70. Some prisoners are stone crazy. They've killed before and have no problem killing again. These types of convicts operate without any regard to human life. You might think that these types must be those sentenced to life. But that's not always true. Anyone is capable of flipping out in such a hostile environment and taking a life or turning someone into a victim who he wishes was dead.

71. There are sexual harassment policies in jail. There are signs posted within the jails and prisons with the numbers of hotlines you can call if you're a victim or if you know of someone who is.

72. Prison yards provide the opportunity for recreation, exercise, fresh air, and smoking (if it is permitted). But make no

mistake, with so many prisoners in one place, anything can and does happen.

73. COs often look for weak prisoners to turn into confidential informants. This trap is usually set by an officer who gets the weak prisoner a good job with top prison pay. In return, the prisoner tells everything he's asked and sometimes more.

74. In male prisons, there are gay male COs. For some of them, this is a dream job.

75. Although staff and the administration are supposed to be professional, unfortunately, that's not always the case. Once COs feel comfortable with individuals or have a particular situation sized up, they tend to bend the guidelines in their favor.

76. Anything can be used as a weapon in prison, including extension cords, television and radio cords, ripped sheets, and clothing.

Pencils, ink pens, the sharpened handle of toothbrushes, screwdrivers, and kitchen utensils are devices prisoners use to stab someone. Loose razors, lids from tuna cans, and materials like soap, locks, and batteries inside sweat socks are also used to cause harm. And hot liquids have been used to scorch.

77. Indigent prisoners receive a care package once a month, which include some basic hygiene products, such as a tube of toothpaste, a razor and deodorant.

78. Some prisoners are always looking for a come-up. A prisoner or group of prisoners that are looking for a score will do so at anyone's expense, even yours.

79. With each day in prison, a new realm of possibilities exists. You never know who's having a bad day. Remember that anyone is potentially dangerous at any time.

80. There's an old adage in prison that states: "If you can bluff them, you can beat them."

81. Single cell status, which means a prisoner is assigned to a cell of his own, can be an honor or indicate a security risk. To achieve the honor, prisoners must maintain a certain behavioral level. Those deemed security risks are separated from other inmates or placed in the hole.

82. Mental health patients that require special treatment are also housed in single cells and monitored by cameras that are inside their cells.

83. One thing that staff and prisoners have in common is

they all get to study human behavior up close and personal.

84. Prisoners lose loved ones while incarcerated and, most times, are not permitted to attend the funeral. Some states do allow prisoners to attend the viewing, but they will be handcuffed, shackled, and escorted by COs or sheriffs. Sometimes prisoners incur the cost for a sheriff's escort and if the prisoner can't afford to pay it, the prisoner is unable to attend.

85. Some prisoners do their time by staying out of the way and playing the role of the model inmate just to ensure early release. But many times, these prisoners are not truly reformed.

86. Some prisoners start their own black market grocery store, which works on a two-for-one or three-for-two basis. For instance, you pay back two bags of chips for one bag they advance, or three-for-two. Be mindful that these activities are against the prison's borrowing and lending policy.

87. Most prisoners eligible for parole try to get in position and stay in position by doing the things that are required of them so they can meet the parole criterion.

88. Prisoners that are serving long sentences or even life sentences might not be eligible for parole, but some attempt to abide

by the prison's rules to get into the position to receive a good classification. Classification is the process where administration determines what custody level you will receive, including minimum, medium, or maximum.

89. A prisoner's custody level can determine the amount of privileges they are allowed to receive within a select time frame. For example, two phone calls a week vs. two phone calls a day, or the type of building where you're housed (minimum, medium, or maximum security).

90. Water used in prisons is recycled. Water from the showers, sink and toilet is treated and returned to the system.

91. Filters are rarely changed in the sinks and water fountains.

92. During the course of your incarceration, people you may not have heard from in years may pop in and out of your life.

93. Depending on the custody level, prisoners may be allowed to receive contact visits, or visits may occur behind glass with a telephone.

94. Some prisons are overcrowded and can't pass inspection by the Fire Marshall. However, they often opt to pay the fine to

continue operating.

95. Some prisons allow prisoners to purchase televisions for their jail cells and even pay for basic cable service.

96. Some prisoners exaggerate their street status in hopes of acquiring unwarranted jail credibility.

97. A hope for lifers and long-timers is that new laws will be enacted in their favor or that they will be transferred to a better prison where there are more opportunities, benefits and privileges.

98. Jail is easy to get into and hard to get out of. There are plenty of envious, hateful people who would like to prevent you from going home.

99. All lifers can't be stereotyped as bad. Some have repented to their God and are sincerely reformed. They truly deserve a second chance.

100. Some people come to jail weak and then become strong.

Some people come to prison strong and then turn weak. Just like in life, jail is what you make it. Remember when that door shuts behind you, you're in a different world!

CHAPTER SEVEN

Things you should know about Probation and Parole

While prisons in different states operate under different rules and guidelines, for the most part, it goes like this:

Say you're serving a 3 to 5-year sentence, you'll be eligible for parole around the time of your minimum release date, which is between six months before or six months after your third year of incarceration. Your parole agent will gather your paperwork and check your file for any reports on you (good or bad), which is why it's important for you not to get write-ups, misconducts or other infractions when you're trying to make parole. They will formulate a pre-recommendation that they will pass on to the parole board. Although the suggestions your parole agents have are persuasive, the parole board has the final say.

If there was a victim in your crime, the victim could attend your parole hearing or send their input by way of victim advocate. Most of the time, when there's a victim involved, your chances of an early release are slim. However, there have been occasions when victims have forgiven the offender and testified on their behalf at the parole hearing.

After your hearing, you will return to your housing unit and await the decision rendered in your case. This decision can take weeks or even months, depending on how backed up the system is. Some components that factor into the ultimate decision include your criminal history, age, employment, family support in society, job skills, adequate housing upon release from prison, prison file, mental health, physical health, and initial charges. There are many other factors; these are only a few.

Now let's say you've met the criteria for parole on or around your minimum date, you will be released from the custody of the state department of corrections (DOC) into the custody of probation and parole. You will usually have to report within 24 hours of release.

Perhaps you did not meet the criteria to receive an early release on your minimum parole date. Then you will receive what's known as a "hit," which means you should try for parole again in three months, six months, one year, etc. This is where the five years comes in on your 3 to 5-year sentence; five is the tail, the back end of your sentence.

You can try to make parole anytime between that minimum

three-year and maximum five-year sentence. Of course, the parole board can opt to max you out.

When you "max out," either the parole board tells you to do your entire term with no early release, or you decide, for whatever reason, that you don't want an early release and you opt to do all of your time. Other than maxing out, the parole board has the authority to decide whether to release you between your minimum and maximum date.

Some states have done away with parole. They use a sentencing system called Truth in Sentencing (TIS), which means you must do 85 percent of your time to be eligible for release; there's no early parole. Some states still have Good Time Earned Time, which means you might only have to serve 28 days on a month, and you can also earn extra days off a sentence by participating in school, work and/or treatment programs.

Depending on your case, POs (Parole Officers)can administer certain conditions. For instance, for drug-related offenses, you can be subjected to more random urine analysis and be required to participate in a select number of Narcotics Anonymous meetings, usually 90 in 90 days. If they determine that your program should be more stringent, you could be committed to an in-house drug rehabilitation center program.

If you're on probation or parole for an alcohol-related offense, such as driving under the influence or public drunkenness, your restrictions may include staying out of bars, night clubs or anywhere where alcohol is served. A 12-Step program through Alcohol Anonymous might also be required.

For certain sex crimes, you would be required to register with the state police and into the Megan's Law database. As a result, there is a serious possibility that community residents would learn about you and object to your living in their community. There are some programs for sex offenders but participating in them exposes their identity to that community.

Generally, having no police contact is a rule that is taken seriously. They figure that if you're having police contact, you're in the wrong place at the wrong time doing the wrong thing. In most cases, this is true. However, there are instances when you could be a passenger in a vehicle that has been pulled over for a routine traffic stop. If the police run your name through their computer and you're on probation or parole, you could undergo further scrutiny.

101

And it will automatically show up in the probation/parole system. If this should happen to you, you should immediately report the incident to your PO. Most of the time, they appreciate the honesty and show some leniency. If you don't report it and they find out from the police or a random probe on the computer, you can believe you're in for some extra trouble.

If you're confronted, don't lie! If they ask, they already know. And if it is something that is insignificant, you'll make out with just having to provide a decent explanation. You may get a verbal warning or some a smack on the wrist. If the police contact consists of something more incriminating, you should get mentally prepared because you're on your way back to prison.

Probation and parole are very strict and intense when it comes to enforcing the rules, regulations and guidelines. This high level of enforcement is designed to give the community some sense of safety.

You're classification as high risk, average risk or low risk will determine the level of probation/parole you undergo. The average and lower levels experience less scrutiny than the higher levels. Another level referred to as Zero Tolerance denotes if you so much as litter or jaywalk and your PO finds out about it, you're on your way back to jail.

On some other levels, for minor infractions, you can receive verbal reprimands, warnings, counseling, treatment, etc. However, if you're on the Zero Tolerance level, that doesn't necessarily constitute that you will remain at that level during your entire period of supervision. As months or years pass, your levels can be decreased as long as you are doing what's required of you and stay out of trouble.

The main requirements of probation/parole include maintaining gainful employment; being where you are supposed to be at curfew; remaining drug-free; participating in any groups, meetings, or recommended treatment programs; paying all court costs and fines; having no police contact; making all scheduled visits to probation/parole; and showing proof of valid driver's licenses, vehicle registration, and insurance if you're the owner of a motor vehicle.

Sometimes POs stipulate special conditions. For example, if you're on probation or parole for a drug offense (any crime related to buying, selling, or using illegal narcotics), you might not be allowed to carry a cell phone. Although today people of all ages carry cellular phones if for nothing more than to keep communication and play with the gadgets that are included on them, you may not be able to carry one if you have a drug charge. Another example is if you were arrested for your offense at 2 a.m., you're more likely to have an early curfew at the start of your supervision. The average time of curfew is 10 p.m. This means you must be at your probation/parole approved residence, the PO will call or possibly make a surprise home visit, so it is in your best interest to be where you're supposed to be at curfew time.

There are two exceptions to the curfew rule: (1) your place of employment conflicts with your curfew, or (2) you're considered low risk and you're not even given a curfew. Unless you're classified an extremely high risk, the POs are usually flexible with work schedules. After all, a huge part of becoming a productive member of the community again revolves around obtaining gainful employment.

As the months pass and you prove that you're able to adapt to society again, you former offenders who are on probation or parole and have a curfew will be given more independence or should I say, "more rope to hang yourself."

Believe it or not, if you're on probation or parole, you're not allowed to quit a job without either having another one lined up or first checking in with your PO. POs look at quitting a job as a sign of irresponsibility. They believe that whatever issues you have with your place of employment, you should iron out to remain employed with that company. Staying employed with one particular company for a significant period of time is the way to build a positive employment history for future and better employment opportunities.

One of the only acceptable justifications for quitting a job is another higher-paying opportunity that presents itself. But even then, you must always notify your PO.

Most POs won't let you work for yourself. The reason for this is because POs think you could doctor your hours and forge paychecks, ultimately making it too hard for them to track you. They want to be able to have an employer account for your work hours.

Another thing you can't change without a PO's consent: your phone number. One of the main stipulations of parole/probation is that you must have a landline (at the time this book was written) where you reside. POs want to know that you're a phone call away when it's time to check up on you. If you change your phone number without their consent, they will definitely think you're trying to elude them, which could violate the conditions of your supervision and land you back behind bars.

Changing residences is probably the biggest no-no of all.

If you don't get your PO's consent prior to changing your residence, you are actually looking at a fleeing offense. This is very similar to escape offenses and there's a good chance a warrant will be issued for your arrest!

The place where you reside is supposed to be one of the key factors in your transition back into society. This is why the Parole/Probation Department is mandated to screen your potential residences prior to your moving in. However, if you're trying to get your life back together and to walk the straight and narrow, give your PO a call prior to doing any of the things I've discussed here and wait patiently until consent is granted—or not granted.

On the other hand, if you're the type who wants to be a rule-breaker, then you can expect to be on the wanted list. This means not only will the police be looking for you, but the Probation and

Parole Department will be on your heels, too!

Depending on your criminal history, they might want to get you off the streets more quickly than you imagined.

Remember the snitches I mentioned that were inside the jail? Well, guess what? Some of them are now on parole too and we know a leopard never changes its spots. You can count on the POs asking them to squeal on you if they see you in passing. You must make the choice if it's worth it or not to go against the grain. But I'll give you a hint: if you do, the odds will not be in your favor!

There are POs who simply want to put in their hours—no more, no less! If you stay out of their way, they'll stay out of yours. Of course, they have their picks, but for the most part, they treat everyone the same.

If you're on parole, you must complete the full term of your sentence. However, probation is the period of supervision after the completion of your sentence or prison term. If you're on probation and you consistently display a positive adjustment in your transition back into society, the POs (Probation Officers) have the authority to take your case back in front of your sentencing judge on your behalf.

If you are employed full-time and have been on that same job for a significant period of time, have always submitted clean urine samples, have never missed a curfew call or office visit (without being excused), and have at least half of your probation time in, you're a good candidate for early release from probation. There's a good chance, with your POs recommendation, that the sentencing judge will suspend the remainder of your probation period. That means if you get in any more trouble, he could still impose your old probation again on top of whatever happens with the outcome of your new trouble, or he can take an educated risk and terminate the remainder of your probation.

A lot of times, probationers don't even know that these possibilities exist, so they end up serving their entire probationary period. And if your PO is engulfed with a giant caseload, these options can easily be overlooked.

Parole

The difference between probation and parole is that parole is an actual part of your prison term. It's the paperwork side of your sentence. You will still see officers except they aren't COs, they are parole officers (POs). Your behavior will still be monitored and observed by the PO, only instead of monitoring it from the controlled environment of prison, they will monitor it through visits to your home, motor vehicle, employment documents (such as work hours and paycheck stubs), cell phone, bank statements, and any other paper or electronic trail you can think of. You must also make visits to their office and be where you're supposed to be at curfew calls. Don't think about being slick with curfew calls by having your sister tell your PO that you're asleep and can't get to the phone when you're actually at a party. POs are not stupid. They undergo immense training.

With parole, you're doing prison time; you're just finishing the end of your sentence back in society. Your time doesn't stop running when you leave prison. Each day, week, month and year you serve on the outside is credited towards your sentence.

Let's say you only have six months left on your parole before you finish your sentence. And let's say you decide to make a foolish decision, like use drugs or stay out past your curfew. Your parole officer would charge you with violating parole and send you back to prison on what's called a "technical violation" or "Tech." At the most, you would be required to do the remaining six months of your sentence in prison and at the end of that six months, your sentence would expire. There would be no additional time added for the technical infraction. The punishment is to extract you from society again and put you back in the slammer.

However, if you commit a brand new offense with only six months left on your sentence, you will still receive credit for the time you serve for your original sentence (the 3 to 5). But you will still have to serve the time that you get for your new case separately. This means that if you're back in jail with six months remaining on your initial case and start with a new case, the six months left on your old case will not be deducted from your new case. And the time on your new case will not begin until you finish serving the time remaining on your original case.

The residence in which you are paroled to must meet parole's standards. They are particularly concerned about residences that are in a drug community or a high crime area. This means that even if you've lived in that neighborhood on that same street your entire life, but parole doesn't see it as a fit environment, they have the authority to refuse to allow you to be paroled there.

No matter whether you resided in an upper, middle or lower class neighborhood, if your residence is considered unacceptable, you will not be allowed to be paroled there. They don't want to encounter any safety or security problems when POs make home visits. And whenever parole is concerned, they prefer to place you in an environment where it feels there are fewer negative influences.

Home Visits

Home visits are scheduled and are randomly conducted.

POs may remind you of DEA or FBI agents. They wear jackets with probation, and parole insignia, bulletproof vests, walkie-talkies, and have handguns in their holsters.

They usually bring two or three officers to your residence unless they are planning to take you back to prison on a technical violation. In that instance, they'll bring even more officers with them.

If you own the property where you reside, they have the right to search your entire home at random. However, if someone else owns it, then they can only search the room you occupy and your personal belongings. If they see, smell, or hear any

111

suspicious activity in the residence and believe you are in some way connected, they can very easily come back with the police and a warrant to search the entire property, regardless of whose property it is.

If they take you back to prison, your time will continue while they figure out what they're charging you with, and the number of days you spend in prison will be credited towards your term.

Probation

Probation is similar to parole with regard to the rules, as well as the amount of scrutiny you'll undergo. The difference between probation and parole is that probation is attached after your incarceration term is completed in full; parole is a part of an actual prison term.

Probation and parole are both ways to monitor a former offender once they're released back into society.

Suppose you've received two years' probation and have successfully been on probation for 18 months with only six months left to go. You do something as minor as commit a traffic violation or as major as committing another offense, the parole

112

board will not throw you in jail. You will have to appear in court and be resentenced for your new offense. You could receive more time or less time than you started with, depending on the severity of the crime. And the 18 months that you received on probation doesn't count for anything. In other words, you are not credited for that time toward any new time you receive.

While there is a difference between the probation and parole systems, the two departments operate as one agency.

Halfway Houses

A halfway house is a residential facility owned either by the DOC or a private company. Halfway houses are for people who make parole but have no residence to be paroled to, or they have a residence that doesn't meet parole's standards. They are also for prisoners who make parole but are considered "high risk." And instead of releasing them back into the community, they are required to stay at a halfway house, which is designed to help with the transition from prison back into society.

If you're in a halfway house, that means you're halfway in jail and halfway in society. You'll live at the halfway house and there will be rules, counselors and COs, except the COs will be plain clothed. It's pretty much like prison, except that you'll be allowed out into the community to search for work, attend a treatment program, visit family members, and participate in other privileges.

While some former offenders take advantage of the adjustment assistance and complete the required assignments, obtain employment and make a successful transition into society, others are weak-minded and choose to run. Because there's a level of freedom, a number of those returning home to halfway houses do not handle that responsibility responsibly.

It's not hard to go on the run from a halfway house, there's no big TV jail break involved. You can abscond when they let you out into the community. Of course, a warrant will be issued for your arrest immediately!

50 QUESTIONS

What are the 50 questions you should ask someone returning home from prison?

These questions are not written in any particular order and you shouldn't bombard someone who just came home from jail with all 50 questions at one time.

However, within the first 30 days of their return, ask them. They're also excellent questions for family and friends to get reacquainted with a loved one. Some of the questions are profound, but all are relevant if you'll be dealing with a former offender in some way.

Of course, there are many more questions to be asked, especially on a personal level. But these are just a few ice-breakers that are guaranteed to get you a front-row seat inside the mind of someone who just came home from jail.

1. What do you plan on doing with your life now that you're out of jail?

2. Do you have any probation or parole, or are you currently under any aftercare supervision?

3.   Do you have any employment lined up?

4.   Where do you plan to work? What kind of employment are you seeking?

5.   Do you have any significant job skills, or did you learn a trade while you were incarcerated?

6.   What was jail like?

7.   What, if anything, did you learn from your experience?

8.   Do you regret doing what it was you were convicted of?

9.   Was it hard for you to do the time? If so, in what ways?

10. How is your credit? If it's bad, do you have plans to rebuild it?

11. Do you miss anything about jail? If so, what?

12. If you could take the whole experience back, would you?

13. Do you plan to further your education? If so, how?

14. Were you on street drugs or alcohol prior to jail?
     Are you in recovery?

15. Have you had drug/alcohol treatment and counseling? Do you think it is working for you?

16. Were you ever overcome by peer pressure?

17. Have you ever been raped in jail?

18. Are you gay?

19. Did you ever have a homosexual encounter?

20. How did you deal with your hormones in jail?

21. What did you do to pleasure yourself?

22. Have you ever contracted any diseases? If so, which ones?

23. Have you been tested for diseases since you've been out of jail? If so, which ones?

24. Did you get any tattoos while you were in jail?

25. How was the tattoo equipment sterilized?

26. How is medical care in jail?

27. Did you get hurt or injured in jail? If so, in what way?

28. Do you think you can stay out of jail now?

29. Do you feel as though prison has institutionalized you?

30. Who supported you financially while you were in jail?

31. Did you miss your family, friends and loved ones? How much?

32. Did you meet anyone in prison that you plan to stay in contact with now that you're out of jail?

33. Where do you plan on living? How long do you plan on living there?

34. Did you find God or religion in jail?

35. Do you feel a sense of freedom again now that you're out of jail? If not, explain how you feel and why.

36. How did your peers treat you in jail?

37. How did the corrections officers and staff treat you?

38. Are you in a gang?

39. Were you in a gang?

40. Was the jail sanitary?

41. Now that you are out of prison, do you think people will look at you differently? If yes, how and why?

42. Has prison changed you in any way? If yes, how?

43. Will you think twice before committing another crime?

44. Did you lose any loved ones while you were incarcerated?

45. How are your friends and family treating you now that you're home?

46. Are you going to take advantage of your second chance? If

yes, in what ways?

47. Do you plan on becoming a part of the problem or the solution in your community? How?

48. Have you accepted responsibility for your crime?

49. Do you feel any remorse for your crime? If so, in what ways?

50. What is the first thing you did when you came home from jail?

About the Author

Veteran author Daron "Timeless Thomas" Swann is no stranger to literary arts... The Wilmington, Delaware native grew up singing with a local neighborhood band... It was through this experience he mastered the ability to transform his thoughts and articulate his message so that it would effectively reach the audience he intended to target...

Thomas was raised in a fairly middle-class neighborhood; however, he unfortunately became a victim of peer pressure and began frequenting the more impoverished side of the community, which eventually became his new home... Trial and error was the method that pushed him towards growth and development... His hierarchy, for the most part, was non-conventional and very much unrighteous...

Seeking a quality of life that's paralleled his upbringing, he always had the bar set a little higher than the rest, but life was moving much faster in the meaner streets of Wilmington, so decision making quickly became a trait that Daron had a hard time mastering...

As with anybody, life had its ups and downs for Daron, but it seemed like "downs" would find him way more than "ups"...Throughout his life journey, he often became no stranger to tragedy and trauma, which really was not conducive for his mental health however one man's problems has no bearing on the way the Earth would revolve...

In the late 1980s, throughout the mid-1990s, the stop-and-frisk laws were in effect all over the country and the local police viciously enforced them with no regard for any citizen who appeared to look suspicious... These borderline illegal searches and seizures not only violated one's constitutional rights, but little contrabands would get retrieved and officers would often turn a citizen into a potential criminal by arresting them for the smallest of offenses... For the Young man and women of color in the urban community back then, running from in eluding law enforcement became a way of life... Consciously and subconsciously, every time we walked out of our doors, we knew that the ones who swore to protect and serve us were out to make the jails overcrowded with our bodies on the count... Sure some slip through the cracks; however, as with the rest of politics, statistically, they needed to make their numbers, so most of us looked at jails as our home away from home...

It was late 2005 when I got arrested for what would be the last time in my life...Growing up going in and out of jail, I was just about tired of repeating the cycle... All those I will admit to contributing to recidivism, I was in my thirties now and it was time to grow up because I did not want to spend the rest of my life expelled from society in the bandages of government institutions... I ended up doing a very significant amount of years incarcerated. However, this changed me for the better; I can honestly say I rehabilitated myself mentally... Once I was released from prison on parole, I enrolled in college and obtained an associate degree at Community College of Philadelphia... That was one of the best moves I've ever made in my adult life because it helped make my transition back into the community real smooth... I mentor plenty of youth and I still do up to this day. I also put together a Ministry of love and spiritual healing for the elderly... My own father was now in bondage at a retirement home and as I would go see him for visits, the smiles of the other clients and patients that resided there would illuminate the entire facility creating an atmosphere of Love, Peace, Grace and harmony each time I was blessed to be in the presence hope our forefathers...

I wrote this book from my soul, intending to help each person who reads it in one way or another. I'm guaranteeing you will become well-informed of the ins and outs, causes and effects, problems, solutions and the questions and answers that exist behind the Gates behind the Walls into the buildings on the tiers and in the jail cells of the prisons across the United States of America.

Contact information:

Website: www.timelessthomas.com

Email: bigdeezyy@gmail.com

JAZZY KITTY PUBLICATIONS
DISCOVERING YOUR TRUE VOICE, PUT IT INTO TEXT!!!
WRITE A BOOK

Jazzy Kitty Publications provides you with the book publishing services you need to become a self-published author. When you come to Jazzy Kitty Publications, you are in need of professional guidance and help to publish and market your book.

Our services are not free but are fair and very reasonable. Your book will be distributed by Ingram Book Group and will be added to all brick and mortar databases, online bookstores, i.e., Amazon.com and Barnes and Noble.com and more. We offer e-publishing, and we will convert your book title into an eBook. **And of course, we also have book/business marketing and promotion available!!!**

FEEL FREE TO CONTACT US
anelda@jazzykittypublications.com
www.jazzykittypublications.com
877.782.5550 x 1001 or Option 1
www.facebook.com/jazzykittypublishing
www.twitter.com/jazzykittygreet
www.instagram.com/jazzykittypublications/